A Place Called In-Between

A Place Called In-Between

Dr. Mary L. Haralson

A Place Called In-Between
Copyright © 2014 Dr. Mary L. Harrison
B. Global Publishing

All Rights Reserved. No part of this publication may be reproduced in any form or by any means, without written permission by the author and publisher.

ISBN: 9780988786677

First Printing October 2014
Printed in the United States of America

Dedication

*To My Brother
Elder Ronald Ross*

Acknowledgements

I want to thank people that sacrificed themselves in some way to help me to give birth to another tool that is designed to bring deliverance to others. Help that was given through prayer, encouragement, and financial contributions, I am truly grateful.

I would like to acknowledge the love and support of my family through their faith in me and their prayers. They have always supported me in doing what I felt God was leading me to do. My six children (The Six Pack), James, Tina, Michael, Monica, Steven, and Timothy, who always gave me the strength to know that I could do whatever I felt led by God to do. Also my grand and great-children (The Little Colas), who keeps me inspired. To my son Steven for using his gifting in art to draw and design the cover for this book, I say thank you.

I would like to thank the publisher, Pastor Riccardo Harris, for his encouragement, his faith, support, and patience shown to me.

To my pastor, Apostle Sharon Rogers and the intercessory team for continuing to keep me covered, thank you. Be blessed.

Contents

Introduction

1.	The Beginning	17
2.	Struggling	25
3.	Trust	35
4.	Waiting	45
5.	Giants	53
6.	Process	61
7.	The Ability to Discern Jesus	69
8.	Day Star Arise	77
9.	Looking in the Mirror	81
10.	Facing Your Brokenness	93
11.	By Faith Follow	105
12.	God's Mandate	111
13.	Overcoming Doubt	119
14.	Know thyself	125
15.	Desire	139
16.	My Battle With An In-Between Place	145
17.	Take the Time to Pray	159
18.	Pain and Forgiveness	169
19.	Transformation	177
20.	Crossing to the Other Side	187

Introduction

Have you ever wondered why? Why, when it seems like things are going well or you seem to be moving forward and just maybe you can finally know that Jesus is with you in what you are striving to do for Him that, things change? It is the whys in our lives that cause the children and servants of the most high to many times feel unsure as well as uncomfortable. Why is it at the time you think you trust what Jesus is speaking in your spirit and that you are moving in that direction, a storm will arise? You know within yourself that He has said let us cross to the other side and immediately a wind arise from nowhere right in the middle of a sunny day. You think to yourself things were well, the blessings of the Lord have gone forth, people have been blessed and you have done well. You have seen the Lord bless all those that were around you and now you are moving in the spirit of the Lord at His command to the other side. You have no doubt that He is with you, yet the wind began to blow, why?

Was there something spoken to you by Jesus that you didn't understand or was there something spoken that you didn't do? Why, has a storm arisen out of nowhere? You say to yourself, I know Jesus is with me, I know with everything that is within me that Jesus spoke to me but yet you're in the middle of a storm, why?

Most of the time the first thing God's children, Jesus' followers want to do is to say, why? What have I done wrong? It is a trick of the adversary to get the followers of Christ to doubt that Jesus has truly spoken into their spirit to do something. Doubt is a weapon that the followers of Christ give to the adversary to use against them that works against their faith (you will learn more about that in the pages that follow).

How do we get to the place Jesus want to take us to and yet be in tact, not destroyed by the winds of life? Know that you will arrive at the place that Jesus has spoken unto you to go. My prayer for you as you enter the chapters of this book is that you, through the scriptural passages given in these chapters will learn more how to trust your master in all that he say unto you, not questioning him and asking why, but trusting Him, know that He can't lie and whatever he says that is what will be done.

Many scriptures you may see several times but just know they are there to build you up in your faith and in the way that you decide to trust the one you say that you serve and not always be ready to ask why. Life itself is a journey, a journey into your destiny and as every person set out on their journey the in-between place is where you are traveling as you strive to reach your destiny. There are several levels of your destiny that you will arrive at as you travel with the Lord. Learn to take in every level and enjoy them as you encounter them.

This is not a live, die journey it is the experience mapped out by God just for you. It is the plan he has for your life, a plan of peace and not of evil. Keep in mind that the author of peace is on board with you as you travel. Just because you don't see him does not mean that he is not with you, he is just resting, why don't you.

Allow your mind to travel farther than the pages of this book. Let your minds eye look into the light of the scripture and see what it is that Jesus is trying to show you. It is not in his inability to show you anything it just may be in my ability to write it or your ability to see what he want you to see, but look. Don't be afraid to allow the spirit to take control and carry you to a place in the anointing that is prepared just for you, that in-between place. Each person's place may be just a little different than another's but don't allow the winds and waves to make you fear and not arrive at the place he want you to go, a place on the other side of your natural eye or your natural mind. Jesus want to take you to a place in the spirit that is awaiting you, a place that you will be able to experience the joy and the peace that you have longed for right here on this earth.

Everyone seem to expect their joy and peace to be in a place that has been prepared for them once they have laid their flesh down, a place that does not include being upon this earth. God has not place his people in a place called earth to be miserable with no joy or peace, struggling and awaiting that day when they can be taken out of life's struggles. Earth was made for his people to live upon and to enjoy but the people of God has paved a way of their own through disobedience and rebelliousness striving to please their own flesh through the lust of their flesh that has caused life to become somewhat unhappy.

Jesus has not removed or destroyed any of the things the Father has for his people but it is essential that the children line up to the will of the Father. If you had or have children and you had bought and prepared many beautiful things for your children to enjoy, things that they could have fun with that you know they would be happy with and those same children became disobedient to your rules and were doing things that brought destruction to themselves and everything that represented you and them, would you just ignore it and let them continue their pattern of life and give them full control over all that you had prepared for them to enjoy a full life with. All of this, knowing that they were destroying themselves and their future, what would a truly good, loving, caring, parent do? Would you do nothing and just sit back and watch as your child, the one you love so much and have given your all to make sure that child had everything he/she would ever need, would you not try lovingly to keep the child from destroying all that you have for him/her or would you have rules that have been put in place to help that child to succeed and to help that child follow those rules to ensure their happiness.

A place called in-between is just that, a place, and this place has been given the name in-between. This is a place that, hopefully, will take your mind off your surroundings and put them on Jesus. There is too many times that an individual's surroundings gain more attention than what is actually happening to the individual or who is right there with that person. This place is a place where you move through it by faith, not by what you see. If you allow yourself to focus on what you see or what you think you see you will miss what the master want you to see, those things that are right in your midst but your natural sight has you blinded. II Corinthians 5:7 says "For we walk by faith, not by sight." Jesus wanted his disciples to see him in their mist, calm and resting not worried about anything. Instead the disciples saw waves rising high and a storm that looked as though it could not be contained. The disciple's broken focus caused them to miss the most important thing there. It was power and authority. This power and authority was housed in the body of Jesus, the master. Jesus had the power and the authority to speak peace to the wind and the waves and the elements became obedient to the authority of Jesus.

As you enter the chapters of this book it is important to ask God to help you see the unseen. See those things that your faith will show you; things your natural eyes will not always detect. Your faith in the Lord will take you to that place called in-between to enable you to get a glimpse of the plans he has for your life.

You can't always see with the natural eye, the things that God has for your life and you can't always successfully enter or exit a situation based on what you can see. Scripture tells us "while we look not at the things which are seen, but at the things which are not see: for the things which are seen are temporal; but the things which are not seen are eternal." (II Corinthians 4:18). The aim of the following chapters is to help you look through the eyes of faith and help you, by faith, to arrive at what Jesus call the other side. If you refuse to allow yourself to look through the eyes of faith you will become stuck in your in-between place asking, why. Start by remembering Jesus' words "Let us pass (cross) over unto the other side" (Mark 4:35).

He said let us, therefore he is with you, and what he says will come to pass. Now, by faith, at his words, began your journey.

As you approach the very subject of in-between most people would see the in-between place as the middle and this is the focus for this topic, the middle. Now as you think about the middle look at the fact that should be faced, there is a beginning, middle, and an ending.

While looking at the in-between place hopefully it will become obvious that a person has gone pass the beginning but have not yet arrived at the ending. To finish the journey that you have begun with Jesus let us continue moving forward that you may arrive at the place Jesus has called each of us to, the other side.

To arrive at the other side says that you have been delivered from your past and you have allowed Christ to launch you forward into the greater in Him and through Him. Don't allow the fear of succeeding to hold you back any longer. The master has called and it is time to go to the other side.

The Beginning

This is truly a book that I am living, as God said that I would, but I'm living it trusting the Lord every day. Much prayer, tears, and anointing is being poured into the pages of these chapters. My prayer is that you can experience the anointing as you read every page and be blessed.

The thing that I would like to convey the most to you, the reader, is every one of us has and will have an in-between place. How we go through that place will determine our strengths and our weaknesses. The in-between place will teach an individual how to build their faith and trust in their savior. Faith and trust are very important in the savior, Jesus Christ.

Most of the time the thoughts that you would think will come to mind when you hear the saying, a place called in-between, would be hard trials and tribulations, all the battles you will face in this in-between place. When winds and waves are present and a storm that you have no power within yourself to control your mind may run to the thoughts of defeat. It is much like the disciples thought when they ran to Jesus and said "Master carest thou not that we perish?"(Mark 4:38).

We in our human frailties see defeat first and Christ, second. Hopefully, you will be able to look at your experience in an in-between place in a different light after you finish this small tool.

This is a tool to help you understand that there will be experiences that come as you take on and go through a process of an in-between place that the adversary would like for you to think you can't overcome. But, I want you to know that we all have a savior, Christ the Lord, that has the power to speak peace to our storms and there will be peace. As long as we walk, run, or react in the spirit of fear to our situations we will not take on the authority that is needed to get what is needed for the situation that we face.

It is important that you not only learn the authority that you possess in the word of God and the spirit of God but also in the name of Jesus. Faith in these will allow you to do what Jesus did. Faith in the promises of the Lord, which is the word of the Lord, is your sword to fight the adversary with. Matthew 21:21 tells you "…If ye have faith, and doubt not … ye shall say unto this mountain, be thou removed, and …it shall be done." It is important and necessary that you believe what Jesus has said you should believe and you will have what he says you will have.

An in-between place is truly a place of spiritual warfare. You have been given a spiritual set of keys to keep with you in your in-between place; these again are faith and trust in Jesus. Keys are given that they be used. There are times the in-between place will present many things, things such as doubt, disappointment, etc. it is important how you handle the in-between place. How you handle that place is based on your faith and trust in God for every step that you take because it is a spiritual war but you are battling in a natural body that is why you have to use your faith in the Lord and keep trusting for every step.

Since you battle from the natural body you will experience anger, hurt, pain, and many other challenging battles of natural feelings and emotions but always remind yourself of who you carry with you in this place of in-between. Whatever the circumstance that surround the events think of who or what it is that you trust the most. You don't wait until a storm come, you enter your in-between place knowing who you trust and make sure you are trusting Jesus as you look toward that place called in-tween.

I'm reminded of Moses when God was preparing to send him unto Pharaoh to tell him to let his people (the children of Israel) go. Moses knew he needed God to be with him in this commission therefore, God said to Moses "my presence shall go with thee" but out of fear Moses' response to God was "if thy presence go not with me, carry us not up hence" in other words Moses was saying to God, if you don't go with us then don't send us, (Ex. 33:14-15).

Fear, despair, and even feelings of being abandoned will make you think you can't make it through your in-between place. God's promise to Moses was the same assurance that Moses gave to the children of Israel, as Joshua was preparing to lead them to the Promised Land, (Deut. 31:6&8). Just like Joshua and Moses you too should take the time to remember who is with you as you enter an in-between place.

A word of advice to those of you who realize that you are in or may be entering a new in-between place, take hope with you. Hope is for your future therefore it gives you expectation to reach the promised destination. God's promised place is in your future not in your past. The only reason you are in an in-between place is because you have left your past, following the spirit of the Lord to your future.

Your in-between place is in the middle of your past and your future. God said "For I know the thoughts I think toward you, saith the Lord, thoughts of peace, and not of evil, to give you an expected end" (Jer. 29:11).

Jeremiah 29:11 opens up a path to hope in your life because it helps you to know that there is a plan for you to have a future planned by God. It is when you make up your mind to truly receive this word of God and seek to follow this path that God's word will continue to give instructions for you to follow. Instructions such as "…be not conformed to this world: but be ye transformed by the renewing of your mind, that ye may prove what is that good, and acceptable, and perfect, will of God" (Romans 12:2). If you will just allow God to lead and instruct you through his word you will see his will and plan for you is perfect. God's will is perfect because his will and his plan for you is Christ in you, the hope of glory, which means in Christ your future is certain. Everything that you may encounter from the time you enter this world until you breathe your last breath is your in-between place. The things you learn or go through, the things you do or don't do is your experience of an in-between place. But still you must keep in mind that you will experience many in-between places and each one is there to help you prepare for the next one. You, precious child of God is so important and you are loved so much that your heavenly father want you to know that you are never alone in this place called in-between. Jesus is with you every step that you take whispering the instructions that you need to make this journey that you are on.

This chapter is called, beginning, just know that we all must start somewhere but you will find that every chapter has in some way instructions, or encouragement just to get you through. This is the way our life in this in-between place is. There will be times that you may need just a little instruction to be able to get to the next step, then there may be times and I'm sure there will be, that you may need just a little encouragement to assure you that you can make it through. Though the winds may blow and the rains may come in your life continue to remember that the master of your soul is on board with you, loving you and holding you to take you through to the other side.

There may come times in your travel through this place called in-between that it may seem like the master is some where asleep but all you have to do is remember that the enemy is the father of lies and there will never be a time that the eyes of the Lord is not upon you. His word is available to you for encouragement. Listen to what it says to you. "For the eyes of the Lord run to and fro throughout the whole earth, to show himself strong in the behalf of them whose heart is perfect toward him" (II Chronicles 16:9). Also Proverbs 15:3 is there to give you encouragement and let you know that the Lord is looking out for you, he know what you are going through at every point of your life. Proverbs says "The eyes of the Lord are in every place, beholding the evil and the good."

Whatever happens, and whenever it happens God see and God know every area of your in-between place but he still want you to trust him to take you through. It is Jesus that can command peace for your life but do you trust him to do just that for you. You may not always understand it all but still trust him. He is yet speaking to you but through your spirit you must be able to hear him. Listen, "Trust in the Lord with all thine heart; and lean not unto thine own understanding" (Proverbs 3:5). Don't worry about you, trust Jesus.

As you go through the chapters of this book know that you

may see a repeat of scripture or an encouraging word but just know the Lord is speaking and there will be times as you are reading that you are to be reminded of what you need to get through your place of in-between. If you are broken, struggling, and seeking ways to truly forgive, the Lord is ready to bring you through that in-between place being able to understand God's mandate for your life and not allowing doubt to steer your ship. My prayers are with you in every page and every chapter. When you travel the in-between be assured that it is alright to cry out to Jesus and allow him to wash you with the oil of anointing and blow sweetly upon you with His spirit, refreshing you to continue the journey. This journey in the in-between is one that you can't get away from but you do have the choice of traveling in the ship with Jesus or attempting to swim it alone.

Each of us are put in the place that we are in for such a time as this. A time to behold who Jesus is to you and in you. Your soul (mind, will, and emotion) is seeking something greater than you have ever known, something that will give you peace, that something is Jesus Christ, the Savior. Maybe you too will find yourself, as you read this book, living it. As you read at the beginning of this chapter, how God told me that I would live this book and at his word, my life began changing. I began experiencing unfamiliar areas in my walk with Christ, but I chose to blindly follow, by faith. There have been times that I found myself trying to go back to the familiar but in doing so I found that I didn't fit any longer. Therefore through tears I find myself repenting and allowing Jesus to help me to continue the journey and the process that he has for my life. There have been times that I have cried and felt alone, but then I remember the promise that he will never leave or forsake me. Then, there are times that I feel so loved and comforted; I'm living the book. Through all that come and all that may go I'm determined to get through this in-between place with all that it may present because I want to make it to the other side.

You may think this beginning chapter seem like the ending but what it represents is there are many beginnings in your life, Praise God, and each has its own in-between place. Therefore remember if you will let Jesus be your guide and not try to get ahead but sweetly follow he will make sure that you arrive at the other side. Allow the love of God and the anointing of the Holy Ghost to take you on this journey that the Lord has laid out for your process to the future he has planned for your life in Him. As you proceed remember, you're moving forward.

Struggling

When you are moving forward in the things of God, there is always a struggle to accomplish what you have been asked to do. Struggle is combat, you are warring with your own self as the spirit of the enemy contend with you to make you think and feel like you can't get through because it is too hard. The more you struggle the more you feel like, "who cares anyway", it's like everyone is too busy doing their own thing to worry about you, but, that is the enemy. Yet you continue to struggle.

The adversary has never approached your territory to help you in any way, but to sow a seed of doubt against Christ in your life. Your walk with Christ is centered on your faith in Him. Can and do you trust Him? In Him all his people have a sure foundation, according to II Timothy 2:19. Jesus Christ is that sure foundation, I Corinthians 2:11. Once you know the true foundation the adversary will not be able to sow seeds in your mind that are designed to break your focus on the Lord.

Focus is important in getting through the in-between place, which you are struggling. Broken focus will cause the struggle to become harder than it has to be. Then you will have problems hearing Christ clearly and the winds caused by life's storms will knock you off course.

There are many things that we struggle against in our in-between place as we attempt to carry out the will of Christ. Maybe every area is not a challenge be every person will struggle in one-way or another. Just being able to think on the things that may challenge the followers of Christ, things such as trust, faith, doubt, insecurity, or even hope. Depression, loneliness, rejection and denial do exist among God's people but if you are not willing to be open jealousy will creep into the challenge. These and other areas that may cause you to struggle will be covered because it is in that in-between place that you will struggle the most as you focus on what Christ has for you on the other side.

I remember that God said to me that I would live this book and the struggle, has been great. But I have practiced trusting Him like never before. At one point I felt like changing this chapter but I've always had the saying "find the good in it". It was when I reminded myself of my own saying that I thought if I have to experience this as I write about it, then I will have to finish this chapter quickly. I will write this one very fast and maybe write about God's blessings coming in the abundance, in the overflow, the more than enough blessings. As I began to laugh I thought to myself, girl God has not given you that chapter yet, and I laughed again. What I'm trying to say to you is every one of us must go through whatever God want us to go through without complaint. If it is struggling just trust Him in the middle of your struggle knowing that he will see you through it.

We can't just change our assignment because we don't like what is happening to us at that season of our lives. There is something in the scripture that I found to be very true in this season of my life. This scripture and promise is found in Philippians 4:7 "And the peace of God, which passeth all understanding, shall keep your hearts and minds through Christ Jesus". I have been able to experience that kind of peace because it is His promise, it has been backed also with another one of his promises "Peace I leave with you, my peace I give unto you: not as the world giveth, give I unto you. Let not your heart be troubled, neither let it be afraid" (John 14:27). You must know that no matter how the adversary try to rock your world you can be rocked because this is a peace that even you don't understand but you know it is from the Lord because he promised and He can't lie. Be blessed people of God, be blessed as you receive His promise in your spirit, Hallelujah!!! To the Lord.

It is in the middle of a storm when you are tossed and you have decided that you will trust him, that you are able to give true worship and true praise, the kind that he alone is worthy of. You may be in-between many things but right now at this point in your life still give him praise. Praise your way through this storm because he has promised never to leave you, (Heb. 13:5). Praise him because his love for you is ever lasting, (Jer.31:3). When you reflect back on the word of the Lord, even though you are in the middle of a great storm, but you know Jesus has spoken to you, you ought to be able to give him worship and give him praise. Don't fear the storm follow the promise.

Each of us know struggle, it is a part of our everyday life in some form or another. Every decision that we make with such un-assurance is a form of struggle. When you know God has given you to do something yet within yourself began to experience fear, while you confess that you trust him that too is a form of struggling. Our struggles are determined many times by the way that we handle the decisions we must make and the level of trust we have in God to help us make those decisions.

The thing you should pay attention to about struggling is to not allow yourself to be consumed by the things that are causing you to struggle. The disciples had their master on board with them yet they struggled with fear when the wind and waves arose (Mark 4:38). Remember what the master has spoken unto you, trust in that and not allow your in-between place to become a place of struggle. When you allow yourself to remember who is with you (the master, Jesus) there will be no room for struggling. Jesus promise not to leave you and he can't lie, therefore, why are you struggling. If you are struggling you don't have the peace that you should have. Take time to sort things out. God says he is the author of peace (I Corinthians 14:33) and he gives you that peace (John 14:27), why do you struggle when peace is in your midst.

Do you wonder sometime, will I make it? Can I make it? Is the Lord really with me in this struggle that I'm going through right now. Do you ever wonder why your in-between place seem more complicated than someone else or why the winds and waves seem stronger in your struggles than someone else does. Well, it is time to trust in the one who know best for you and will not leave you alone in your time of struggle, but will make a way for your escape (Prov. 3:5; Heb. 13:5b). Struggle is never easy but it is very important to trust the one who know all and especially what is best for you to bring you into a place of being able to recognize how to get through not just one but every struggle. It is Christ that will bring you through when you have an unwillingness to be obedient; you will find this as a place where your struggle began. Your willingness to move in blind obedience to the spirit of the Lord will cause him to speak peace in your life and your struggle will subside. God will not lie, therefore you don't have to worry about trusting him to do just what he say, but can he trust you to move in blind obedience to his word. Learn how to talk to God with a sincere heart. Tell him, speak to me Lord and I will hear, draw me and I will run after you. Lord, whatever you say that I will do, this is blind obedience. This is the place that he want us to get to and when you can learn how to do this he will speak peace and command your struggle to be still just as he did with the storm in his disciple circumstance as they crossed to the other side. Struggle is there to make you question or doubt what Jesus has spoken unto you as though he cannot or will not preform his plan and his promise for your life. The adversary want the people of God to doubt his ability to bring them out. This will allow doubt to become a weapon for him to use against the people God. I used to say, "God said it, I believe it and that settles it." I had to learn it was not about me believing it for it to be settled. The truth is God said it and that settles it. Whether we choose to believe it or not, It does not mean God's word is not true. When God speak it shall be so.

There are times that people use their struggles with self-pity to get attention. If you will learn to rest in the midst of your struggle you will go through so much better. The in-between place is there to take you to the other side of your struggles, healing, doubts, tears, and any other thing that try to stop you from going where Jesus said go, "let us cross to the other side". Where Jesus want to take you the multitude can't follow. You must be able to let some things go because they will hinder you. There are some things and some people that don't want to follow Jesus, therefore they can't follow where

Jesus want to take you.

When you look at your struggles it would be wise to seek out the reasons why you are struggling. In this place that I call in-between it is a place of many people's struggles. A place where it is important to know who you truly are, where you are and how do you deal with it.

Many times we climb the walls of our mind knowing that there is something more that we feel lead to do but we are unsure how to get it done. We're not sure where to start, we feel lost but yet the urge to do continues to hunt us. We struggle because we are in a place where the moment that we decide to try to walk on the water of being unsure...trying to define ourselves, the winds began to blow. We find ourselves in the middle of a storm that we are, in some ways, afraid to endure. The fear, for me is a reminder of Peter, when he saw Jesus walking on the water asked if he could come to him on the water. Once Peter had Jesus' permission to come his faith caused him to walk on the water but fear of his surroundings, in the place that he was in, caused him to fear and began to sink (Matthew 14:28-30).

Your struggles are not there to make you fear but, to help you to decide if you will trust God to bring you through and help you to become who you were meant to be. Struggles will help you decide if you are willing to move forward by pressing toward the gifts and callings that God has already ordained in you. Struggles were never designed to hinder you but to push you forward. They were designed to give you the opportunity to be strengthened in your faith and your trust in God. Psalm 46:10 says, "Be still, and know that I am God…" Therefore, when you recognize who God truly is in you, you should have no problem trusting him to carry you through the struggles that you are facing. Those same struggles will strengthen you in your journey to the other side of fulfilling every promise of God for your life.

I started this chapter by saying that struggle is combat, can you rely on God's word enough to fight? Psalm 91:11 says "For he shall give his angels charge over thee, to keep thee in all thy ways". Also Genesis 28:15 says "…I am with thee, and will keep thee in all places whither thou goest … for I will not leave thee, until I have done that which I have spoken to thee of". You may struggle for a moment but you have no reason to fear or not trust God. If Jesus said let's cross to the other side, you will arrive at the other side.

It is time for you to tell your faith and tell your mind, we are going to the other side. Let your in-between place know that you are only there for a moment, because you are going to the other side. Speak to yourself and let yourself know that, you may be struggling right now, and you can feel the storm of life with its wind and waves but you are going to arrive at the other side. While you are putting self in check just speak to yourself and tell self what Joshua 1:9 says, it says, "Have not I commanded thee? Be strong and of a good courage; be not afraid, neither be thou dismayed for the Lord thy God is with thee whithersoever thou goest". Tell yourself, therefore self I will put on my garment of praise because, self I am now clear of this fact, the joy of the Lord is my strength and not only will I go to the other side but I have the master (Jesus) in my spiritual ship and I will arrive stronger than ever. Now you ought to give the Lord praise in the Holy Ghost.

Struggles come in this life but keep the faith knowing that God is working his plan in you for an expected end and it will strengthen you if you will allow it. Now that you know how to make it through don't be afraid to allow your process to take place but just let the Lord do what he do. Hopefully you will find the strength in this chapter to reach out and help your brother and/or your sister to make it too. Keep in mind that when one struggle is over another will come. Now that you know the key to your victory, use it.

Trust

Maybe you should come to the realization that the in-between place is a place of struggle. It is the middle of your start and your finish. Until an individual is able to face up to the fact that there may be some form of struggle in just about everything they may face in everyday life, then the ability to hold on and work through the struggles will always be difficult. It will also determine if you are able to get through that in-between place.

There are times as you are going through the in-between place that your struggles will make you feel like your world has been turned upside down. Just know that though the waves are high and beating up against your ship of life you can get through this place when you choose to see it for what it is. The struggles are there to bake your focus on the one who will see you through to the other side. In the mist of this struggle it is important to truly gain insight on who or what you have holding you up in this place called in-between.

Many times it is right in the middle of the struggles that you will have to decide if you are willing to trust the Lord. God gave assurance to Jacob in the middle of his dream saying "behold, I am with thee and will keep thee in all places whither thou goest…for I will not leave thee" (Genesis 28:15). It was also in the New Testament that warnings were given to the people to be content with such as they had also the assurance that the Lord would never leave or forsake his people, (Hebrews 13:5). There are times when people are right in the middle of a struggle that they need to be assured that it is alright to trust the Lord. Keep in mind that your ability to wait and wait with peace will show your ability to trust. I am a witness that if you trust God he won't let you down.

Trusting is not as easy as it might seem; it comes with a price. Let me say this, anything that you give up to trust God is worth it in the end. God is just waiting on each of us to let him work for us, to move in our behalf. He want to make your days lighter and the struggles much lighter, but above all you have to trust him to do it for you. Trust comes with making a choice. The prophet Elijah spoke to the people that were with Ahab and said "how long halt ye between to opinions?" (I King 18:21) There are times that making a choice is necessary and no one else can make it for us but we must do it for ourselves. The step to trust God has to be done on your own. The willingness to trust will be there as you

activate your faith. I have been teaching that your faith is the realization of what you don't see. It would not be faith if you were able to see many of the aspects of this in-between place. Faith will be in the mist of your ability to do. You may say, "do what?" when someone ask you to make a step into a realm that you can't see with your natural eyes, but you will take the step of following Jesus' command with peach. Peace was not what the disciples had when Jesus spoke, "Let us pass over unto the other side" (Mark 4:35). When Jesus speaks something happens and for his disciples it was a storm and their peace and their trust evaded them for a few moments. Their response to Jesus was "Master, carest thou not that we perish?" (v. 38), when you trust you won't question. Jesus responded to the disciples "…how is it that ye have no faith?" in other words Jesus was asking, why don't you trust me? When you learn to trust it will remove doubt. Doubt will give Satan a weapon to use against you. You need to look back over your past and take inventory to see if you have been exercising doubt and walking in fear, or have you walked trusting Jesus by walking in the authority that is yours when you trust the Lord. Take time right now and decide what you have been doing, not what you have been saying that you were doing but what has really been going on in your walk with Christ.

Have you really trusted every promise in the word of God? While walking in that authority it could bring doubt or uncertainty to your mind. Have you found that you have been doubtful and operating in fear along the way? Well, if doubt and fear has filled a large space in your life it is not too late to repent and start again. Acknowledge that you need Jesus' help then allow him to do what he does best, give you a new beginning, one with peace and love wrapped in faith and trust. When you truly love the Lord you will trust him, He will not fail you. If you are going to trust him why allow doubt to fill your heart and mind in every situation that you encounter. You may not always understand or agree with the situation but it is important to trust the Lord to do what is best for you. Began trying to truly understand that God will not lie and he truly love you, it will enable you to trust him without question. Because you will not always understand everything about the move of God in your life, the word of God encourages his people not to depend on what they understand to make every decision. Proverbs 3:5-6 says "Trust in the Lord with all thine heart; and lean not unto thine own understanding. In all thy ways acknowledge him, and he shall direct thy paths." It is your trust in Jesus that will get you to your destination safely, even when the winds and the storms of life are raging. Continue to remember, whatever Jesus speak he will perform, trust him.

Trust will not allow you to second guess what the master has spoken to you. When Jesus said "let us pass over unto the other side" (Mark 4:35), the faith that is locked up in side of you will not let you doubt, but will open the trust that you seek to use in the situation, to know that what he had promised (spoken unto you), he was able to perform, (Romans

4:21). Yes, he is concern that you think that you are perishing but he want you to trust him to do what he has said. Now open yourself up, let go and allow yourself to pass over to the other side just as the master has said. Reassure yourself that the master of the sea is riding through the storm with you; therefore, you have no need to worry or fear just trust him. Be assured that it has never been God's intent that anyone becomes stagnant in any situation that you have chosen to trust him in. When you left the shores of a place called here, headed to a place called there, it was the master's will that you arrive with your faith, your trust, and your expectation intact. There is such power in your faith when you use it to trust your savior it can only lead to expectation and that expectation will be fulfilled. Come on now with all that is within you trust him. God will speak to you as he did to me. Now, let me share with you my go through in this season of an in-between place as I sit here. I can feel the winds are blowing much harder than they have blown at other times, but in a different way. One thing that I can say, at this moment I still have the strength to hold on and continue to trust God's plan for my life. I'm not at the point that I feel my master does not care. Although I can't swim naturally so, this is a spiritual battle and my spiritual ship is really rocking but I know my master has this in His control. I heard the Lord speak into my spirit on one occasion and to my amazement he said, "I got this" even now I can still feel his "I got this" assurance. But I still want my ship to stop rocking and the hard winds to stop blowing.

Allow me to say this if you will, trust is not always easy but it is a choice and I choose to trust Him (Christ, the Lord). It is in Him that I live, move, and have my being (Acts 17:28a), therefore, I yet choose to trust Him. I'm striving to learn how to lay back in his arms, relax, and ride the waves of my storm out. It has been said that you should not fight against the water if you don't know how to swim. If you will let yourself relax you will be able to float. Therefore, if the waves are high in a situation that you may have (spiritually) don't fight against your situation learn how to call on the author of peace, the one that came that you might have peace in him and through him. You will grow tied and weary trying to spiritually swim against the tides, therefore relax in the arms of Jesus and prayerfully allow Him to bring you out with peace and your joy intact. No situation is too big and no problem to heavy for out father and redeemer of our soul to handle, but you got to believe it. Listen to what his words are saying to you. While you are stroking against a wave much bigger than you have encountered before and you are getting tired of doing this on your own, He says "Have faith in God. For verily I say unto you, that whosoever shall say unto this mountain, be thou removed, and be thou cast into the sea; and shall not doubt in his heart, but shall believe that those things which he saith shall come to pass; he shall have whatsoever he saith. Therefore I say unto you, what things soever ye desire, when ye pray, believe that ye receive them, and ye shall have them" (Mark 11:22-24). Your freedom of mind, your peace and your deliverance, that ability to swim out by relaxing and resting in Jesus prayerfully, is based also on your ability to believe. Make a choice, do I sink or do I swim. If you choose to swim, speak to your mountain and tell it to move, because it is blocking the path that leads to the master. When you think about it swimming also takes work. I have been told that in swimming you use all the muscles in your body, therefore it seems as though floating would be much easier. Floating takes relaxing and to relax you must be able to trust in some one or something. Now I ask, will you choose to swim or float? But again keep in mind the choice to float means you have chosen to relax which mean you are choosing to trust. Proverbs tells us to trust in the Lord with all thine heart; and lean not unto thine own understanding, (3:5). Now, can you trust Him (Jesus) enough to lay back, relax, and float your way out of your storm? When you gain the ability to trust it means that you have some form of expectation. When you trust something or someone to help you to float this mean you believe that same something or someone has whatever is needed to sustain you and keep you from drowning. Scripture says, "now unto Him that is able to keep you from falling…" (Jude 24) this will help you become comfortable or relaxed in what you trust. It is difficult to write about trust without writing about struggle just as in writing about struggle trust was included. As you read throughout the chapters you will find trust included because if you are going to survive this journey, on planet earth, called life and the process of salvation it is necessary to trust the Lord and there will also be some struggles from time to time. The same is true also concerning certain scripture references; there will be some repeats which will help you get them into your spirit. If you can get certain scriptures in your spirit it will help you be equipped for the journey as well as trust God according to his word.

To be able to trust in something or someone is very important but there may be times when you ask yourself, who can I trust or who better yet, who should I trust? Trust can seem difficult sometime but in just about everything that you do and in almost every area of your life it will require some trust. If your life dose not involve trust in some way you wouldn't have a life. Deciding where to place your trust or even when to trust takes prayer and seeking God for guidance. Being able to relax and believe that God will give you when and where to place your trust is a step that take courage also. As you began to make such important choices remember what the scripture says, "Trust in the Lord with all thine heart; and lean not unto thine own understanding. In all thy ways acknowledge him, and he shall direct thy paths" (Proverbs 3:5-6). Always try to keep in mind that Jesus is the only one that can truly help you to make the right decision. Listen, please keep in mind that when you place your trust in someone or something even after you have prayed, things won't always make you happy. You must learn how to be pleased in the choices you have made especially if you know that you have made the best choice that you could because you put your trust in God first. He makes no mistakes and whatever he leads you to do will always work for your good. Learn to obey. Jesus is the master of the sea and the elements obey him why shouldn't you. What Jesus does is help you move in the right direction and it may not make you feel good but it really will work for your good. God is pleased when you make the decision to trust him with all of your heart. You may not even understand what the Lord gives you to do, but it is not in what you can understand but in the fact that you chose to trust the path the Lord laid out for you. Remember, He love you.

When you walk close to God and trust his direction for your life he will walk close to you, step by step. Don't ever be afraid to trust the Lord but be sure it is him that you are putting your trust in. There is so much to be said about trust but I realize I can't cover it all. There are just a few more things I would like to say in this chapter but keep in mind that through out this book you will continue to read something relating to trust.

Please keep in mind as you pray and feel as though you have the answer for that decision that you are making, trust. Don't give up on your decision to trust, and during those times when you seem confused, trust. When your heart is braking, trust. There will be times when you have prayed and it will yet seem like you don't know what to do, find the strength in your heart to trust. While you are in your spiritual ship trying to make it to the other side, remember that Jesus is with you because he promise not to leave you therefore just trust in that fact, it's his word. While you are facing those that has hurt you the most trust yourself to be able to forgive. After all of your praying and seeking God for the answers has been done and it seem as though the storms of life are higher and higher, and the enemy want you to feel as though all is lost, trust and keep trusting.

Waiting

When you are in your in-between place, you are in the timing of God's process and God's will.
The place of in-between will increase you faith. It is a place of waiting for what God already has planned for your life. If He is willing to wait, we his people should wait also, (Isa. 30:18). God has waited for his people for thousands of years down through time and He through Christ is continuing to wait for his people to return to Him.
It is the waiting in the in-between that builds strength. According to Isaiah 40:29-31, which says, "He giveth power to the faint and to them that have no might he increaseth strength. Even the youths shall faint and be weary, and the young men shall utterly fall: But they that wait upon the Lord shall renew their strength; they shall mount up with wings as eagles; they shall run and not be weary, and they shall walk, and not faint." To wait does not always exemplify patience; the disciples in the ship with Jesus didn't exercise patience when the storm arose. They woke Jesus and said "carest thou not that we perish" (Mark 5:35). They were in the ship waiting to arrive at the other side, but not through patience. Jesus asked them "why are ye so fearful?" their fear drove their patience out.

When the adversary is challenging you learn to wait for your promise with patience. You must be able to recognize that Jesus love you regardless to where you are in your life and he will fulfill every promise that he has spoken to you. He is Omni—present because of his love for you. Trust him at his word and truly learn how to wait on him in patience.

Faith in who Jesus is and his word are two things necessary to have the ability to wait patiently. Although Jesus' disciples walked with him, saw his miracles, and received his teachings, yet when the storm came there arose a fear that over road their faith in how much the master truly cared about each of them and in the things he had spoken. Listen again to what Jesus had to say as his disciple questioned his concern for their safety when a storm arose, "why are ye so fearful?" Their faith in the master's love and concern was shaken and their ability to wait seem to no longer exist.

How do you wait when storms arise in your life, patiently or impatiently? Do you continuously remember the promise of Jesus to never leave you, and never forsake you? Do you have the faith to blindly trust Jesus at his word? There will be times in life, as you serve the Lord, that you will be asked to cross over to the other side of your troubles and disappointments but as you make the step to follow by faith when you get to an in-between place a storm will arise. At this very delicate place in your life do you have the faith to wait patiently knowing what Jesus has spoken shall come to pass or do you become impatient in your waiting and began to believe that your storm is greater than Jesus, the master of your soul.

A key to waiting successfully is to make up your mind that you will get to the other side. This can be accomplished by quoting scripture and remembering the promises of God, scriptures such as "...thus saith the Lord that created the, O Jacob, and he that formed thee, O Israel, (put your name there), Fear not: for I have redeemed thee, I have called thee by thy name; thou art mine. When thou passeth through the waters, I will be with thee; and through the rivers, they shall not overflow thee: when thou walkest through the fire, thou shalt not be burned; neither shall the flame kindle upon thee. For I am the Lord thy God, the Holy One of Israel, thy Savior" (Isa.43:1-3a). Therefore when you choose to remember who you really are you can make ready to start the journey of going to the other side. Without allowing the adversary to make you think that your Savior don't care about you, you stand up, look at your storm and say as the Apostle Paul, "For I am persuaded, that neither death, nor life, nor angels, nor principalities, nor powers, nor things present, nor things to come, nor height, nor depth, nor any other creature, shall be able to separate us from the love of God which is in Christ Jesus our Lord" (Ro. 8:38-39). Where you read us and our, you say me and my. You must be able to allow the word to become personal to you. You may get in an in-between place but just knowing Jesus is the one that truly love you and he cannot lie, according to Numbers 23:19, you will exercise the faith to patiently wait, knowing if Jesus has spoken to you to cross over to the other side, your storm can't stop the move of God to take you to the other side of your little storm. It is only big to you; it is not bigger than Jesus. There is always a "peace be still" in your in-between place no matter how full your spiritual ship may seem it can't sink when the master is on board. Hallelujah! Give God praise.

While you are in a state of waiting, there is always something that will be able to encourage you, found in the word of God. While you are in the position of waiting on God to come through for you, listen to what the psalmist had to say "wait on the Lord: be of good courage, and he shall strengthen thine heart: wait, I say, on the Lord" (Psalm 27:14). The ability to wait should also have a lot to do with who you are waiting for and who you are sometimes waiting with. If you are not in the right company it can be difficult to remain in anticipation for your expectation to be fulfilled.

Sometimes as you anticipate a move of God, self always wants everything right now but the Heavenly Father know that you may not be in the position to handle the blessings you seek at that time. There are some things that God need to work out in you, things and areas that you need to be strengthen in. There are times while you are waiting, you need to learn how to humble yourself. While you wait there need to be a lot more prayers going up before the Lord. Not prayers to say "I want", but prayers to say Lord, I give you praise because you are wholly. I praise you God because you are worthy of praise. Praise Him because he has not left you alone. Give him praise because he has kept you this far and shielded you from the hand of the enemy. It is the Lord that has not allowed your ship to go down and it is he that has allowed you to continue waiting. When you make up your mind that you really don't mind waiting and make up your mind that while you are waiting you will truly give him praise with all that is within you. It is at this point in your life that you can wait without fear and without giving ear to what the enemy wants to whisper to you. Waiting is not always easy but waiting is possible. It is necessary to allow God to teach you how to wait step-by-step and day-by-day.

Take the time to search your heart on why you wait. Are you waiting because you love God and you trust him to do what you need him to do or is it because you have no one else that you can depend on to get what you need? It is important to know for yourself why you do the things that you are doing. Jesus loves his people so much and he wants what is best for them always, shouldn't we love him with our whole heart too. Not just because he has what we need but also because he has shown his love for us through the shedding of his blood, through the sufferings he endured. He laid his life down for us all and it has been revealed to us through the scriptures, which says, "But God commendeth his love toward us, in that, while we were yet sinners, Christ died for us" (Ro, 5:8). Anyone that has proven his love for you through death can be trusted to do what need to be done that you get what you need and keep you safe. Therefore while you are riding through the storm of your in-between place, be patient and wait on the master to bring you through safely. Don't allow your mind to run away with you thinking that Jesus doesn't care about you. If he care about the little sparrow, he care about you.

There are many things in our life that we will have to go through and deliverance doesn't always come quickly therefore we must learn how to wait. Waiting can be a little easier when you truly trust the one you are waiting for. You will remind yourself when doubt try to creep in, that the one you are waiting on will come. When you are able to recognize that the one you are waiting for can't lie, and this person love you more than you love yourself and they have always done what they said they would do and anything that they have ever done for you has always been for your good. Now this is the kind of person that will make you not mind waiting for. The ability to wait is based on why you are waiting.

Giants

While traveling through this in-between place, that you may find yourself in, it is possible that you may encounter what seem like and appear to be giants. In this place you must be able to take a moment and realize that what look like a giant or giants is not necessarily a giant. But, just in case the thing that is challenging you is in all reality a spiritual giant just remember that it is not an undefeatable giant.

Your spiritual giant is not undefeatable because God's word gives his children how to be victorious over the enemy. His word says, "I can do all things through Christ which strengtheneth me" (Philippians 4:13). If you, as a child of God, can trust in His word and not allow yourself to doubt it will become true to you according to your faith. Mark 9:23 says, "If thou canst believe, all things are possible to him that believeth." There will be scriptures that you will read over and over throughout the pages of this book, don't get tired. These scriptures are there to strengthen you and encourage you that you may grow in your faith in the Lord. They are scriptures that will fill your heart and eventually they will fill your mouth so that every time you face a giant in your in-between place you will know how to use the word against that giant and every giant that try to dominate the thoughts of your mind. "For the word of God is quick and powerful, and sharper than any two edged sword, piercing even to the dividing asunder of soul (your mind, will, and emotions) and spirit, and of the joints and morrow, and is a discerner of the thoughts and intents of the heart" (Hebrews 4:12). Now when that giant try to dominate your mind the word of God is there to cut down the very intent of that giant and the giant itself. Giants attempt to gain victory over its prey by taunting them in order to throw their minds off of what they want to accomplish. Now that you are made aware of how God's word can be used to help defeat the spiritual giants that have been sent to try you, hopefully you will be able to recognize the importance of the written word of God.

Now, back to those supernatural taunting spirits. You must be able to realize that you are not the only one that has been taunted by your adversary. Try to remember David when Goliath confronted him. Goliath taunted David saying, "Come to me, and I will give thy flesh unto the fowls of the air, and to the beasts of the field" (I Samuel 17:44). This was just a portion of Goliath's taunting but the fact remain that David was not moved by Goliath for he knew what God was able to do and how God had moved on his behalf before. This is what God's children must do now, they must have faith in the fact that he loves you and he will not leave you alone in the middle of your battles. It is important to keep in mind the kind of God that you trust and have your faith in. The God that is able to do exceeding abundantly above all that you could ever ask or think, based on Ephesians 3:20.

God's children never have to wonder if he is able to fulfill their every need. When you are facing one of your spiritual giants remember the words of the Apostle Paul in Philippians 4:19 "But my God shall supply all your need according to his riches in glory by Christ Jesus". I won't say that you will not face attacks but remember you are not alone with what you face, you must trust in the Lord with all your heart and lean not unto your own understanding (Proverbs 3:5).

Anytime we as the people of God began to rely on our own way of thinking we get in trouble. Trusting in your understanding will most surely cause you to become a victim of your circumstances. Victims see their giants as undefeatable. The victim can never seem to figure out the best solution or which way to go to get away from the supernatural things that are weighing them down. Things that seem so large and so heavy that they become too much to handle, causing their emotions to give into that big, strong, giant.

That giant, yes, this is what the enemy wants you to see your situation as...that giant. It can be defeated from your mind just as David defeated the giant that taunted the armies of Israel. Just look at the giant Goliath, he was known to those in his surroundings, the ones that feared him, as the champion (I Samuel 17:23). But, just look at the way David went before the giant that thought he could cause fear to come upon David by taunting him. First, David had to openly confess that he trust God. David says "…the Lord that delivered me out of the paw of the lion, and out of the paw of the bear, he will deliver me out of the hand of this Philistine" (I Samuel 17:37). David knew that God had delivered him before and faith and trust in God said that he would do it again. Every time a spiritual giant shows up in your circumstances, just call to your remembrance how many times God brought you through. He promised to never leave us nor forsake us. Therefore, because David knew in whom he believe he makes his statement of faith to Goliath. David said "Thou comest to me with a sword, and with a spear, and with a shield, but I come to thee in the name of the Lord of hosts, the God of the armies of Israel, whom thou hast defied" (I Samuel 17:45). When you are being taunted always remember who is on your side. Think of the promises God has made to you. Through your obedience to God you have the promises that he gave to Israel for their obedience too. "Behold, I send an angel before thee, to keep thee in the way…" this gives you assurance that you are not in your situation alone. Now think of another promise God has given his children in their obedience "I will be an enemy unto thine enemies, and an adversary unto thine adversaries" (Exodus 23: 20, 22). It is these promises that you can rely on to gain courage and strength. Tell yourself, God did it before and he will do it again, and then trust what you have said and let nothing cause you to doubt what you have said. You will conquer the obstacles that seem like giants in your life. When you can recognize that God has brought you through various things that it seem like you could not make it through. Your giant seemed so large and so strong; it was like there was no way to defeat this thing. When it seem like your mind can't see pass the giant, tell yourself "I don't care what this look like or feel like, I trust God and this too will be conquered. His word says we are more than conquerors (Ro. 8:37). Now, if you are more than a conqueror you become a victor, Praise God.

David told Goliath "this day will the Lord deliver thee into mine hand; and I will smite thee, and take thine head from thee". Please allow this word to soak into your spirit that you too can become victorious. Then, David with his faith in God "prevailed over the Philistine…and smote the Philistine and slew him…David ran, and stood upon the Philistine, and took his sword…and cut off his head…" (I Samuel 17:46, 50-51). David became more than a conqueror over Goliath, he became a victor, the moment he took Goliath's head off.

It is the season that you must learn how to become a victor in everything the enemy throw at you that seem like a giant, and the key in these event is (seem like). Because something "like seem", does not make it so. If you have faith as a mustard seed you can speak to your mountain and command it to move and it will have to move. A little faith, if you use it, is bigger than any mountain. Precious child of God use your faith and bring that giant or mountain in your life down. Now, if you understand what has just been given to you, give God Praise. David believed God, he trusted in what God could do because he had seen what God had done.

There are giants waiting to challenge the people of God in everything they do but you must know who is in you and who you represent. When you can do this you will not be overcome by what the giant look like. The giant that David was fighting had six toes and six fingers on each hand and each foot giving him a total of twenty-four fingers and toes. Giants are un-natural beings therefore you must recognize that what you are facing many times are un-natural beings. David had been dealing with giants a long time, he even killed Goliath's brother but David had other giants in his path. David's other giants may be some of the giants that you may encounter too, if you have not already. David encountered the giants of temptation, and murder, also the giant of disobedience and many others. But, you can conquer every giant and walk in victory over every giant through the power of God found in His word and the Holy Ghost. The word of

God that was spoken to others is also good for you in your circumstances. God spoke to Zerubbabel in Zechariah 4:6 "not by might, nor by power, but by my spirit, saith the Lord of hosts." By the spirit of the Lord of host you can conquer every giant that stand up in your life. When the children of Israel went into Canaan, their land of promise, there were giants but they had the power to conquer their giants. God had given them the assurance that their enemy would not be able to overtake them. They had the power to defeat the giants in their land. It was their land that God had promised and they didn't just lay down and give up neither can you, you must remember what the Lord has promised you, now get yourself up and fight. God has your back and you don't have to worry, just be determined.

David said to Saul, let no man's heart fail because of him (Goliath), thy servant will go and fight with this Philistine (this giant, this superhuman), I Samuel 17:32. Remember that Goliath may have been superhuman but God is super spiritual. David was not trying to make a name for himself. It was not about David but he said "This day will the Lord deliver thee into mine hand; and I will smite thee and take thine head from thee…that all the earth (everybody) may know that there is a God in Israel, (I Samuel 17:46). You must learn how to trust the promise of God and get yourself up by faith. Take the sword of the spirit, which is the word of God and take the head of your giant off. Keep in mind that Canaan, Israel's promise land, was on the other side of the wilderness, which they had traveled for the past forty years. There were many obstacles and/or giants that the children of Israel had faced during their travel from Egypt until they were able to cross the Jordan and enter Canaan. The fact remained; the many forms of giants they encountered in their wilderness did not overcome those that were obedient. What giants are you facing and what are you going to do about them.

Process

The in-between place is part of a process. This process is designed to take those that will follow, into the plan God has for their lives, (Jer. 29:11). God has a plan for each of our lives but you will not just wake up one day and find yourself in that future he has planned.

The process that you must go through is continuous and as you proceed through this process you will constantly be developed into what God want for you and the things he has for your life. It is the willingness to follow the process that will get you to God's goal for you. Process is not always easy but it is possible. The process will develop every part of you that you will allow.

The Mind

Your frame of mind is very important in the process of your in-between place. As a person thinketh in his heart, so is he (Prov. 23:7). Your ability to think clearly depends on your ability to hear God clearly. You may not always understand what you hear but by faith follow your God given instructions. Continue to remember the process is continuous, many times there will be a changing taking place just for you, allow the change to happen don't fight it. It is the changing that will take place, which will cause your mind to stay alert and not become stagnated.

The mind, your mind, is a very powerful tool that God wants to use to get you through your in-between place. This in-between place that you are in was not designed to keep you there but to transition you from where you were to where God want to take you. Being as powerful as the mind is, you sometime want to know things in advance but don't allow your mind to get you caught up in trying to figure everything out. There are times that you may find yourself caught up in over thinking some things when God only want you to trust him for the next thing that that he want you to do or even the next thing he want you to know.

Every person must keep a willing mind, one that will yield to the voice of God. If you can't or won't yield your mind to the voice of God there will be no peace of mind. Isaiah 26:3 says, "Thou wilt keep him in perfect peace, whose mind is stayed on thee; because he trusteth in thee." It is important to have the peace of God while moving through your in-between place, which makes the sensitivity to his voice better.

There are times we have the tendency to question everything, things such as, how will I know the voice of God? Or how will I know what he is telling me to do? And so forth but trust the mind that God has given you. Remember, don't over think things; your mind will yield to the God that made it.

There are times that a thought will come to your mind like you have never had before or the same thought will come to your mind several times, pay attention to it. There are also those times when in your mind you can just hear something being said, don't be afraid and don't fight it, just relax and God will do the rest. Keep in mind that God has said the thoughts that he think toward you are of peace and not of evil (Jer.29:11), therefore why should you be afraid of the voice of God that comes to help you get through this in-between place that you are in.

Tell yourself I'm going to get through this because I recognize that I can do all things through Christ, he is with me and whatever he is doing in my life at this season is for my good. This in-between place is delivering you from you. Yes, we need to be delivered many times from our own selves. Let the old you go and take on the new you, the one that God has placed a new will in and the determination to press forward like never before. The new you will allow yourself to be stretched from the old into the new. Stretching can hurt but it depends on how you are stretched. I use to take up water aerobics and doing the exercises and being stretched in the water it was very affective for me and while I was being stretched in the water I didn't feel it as much. When I would do stretching exercises out of the water it was uncomfortable but I did them. I look at this example of stretching in and out of water in a spiritual sense.

Either of the two ways given for being stretched can be effective but one way is easier than the other. Stretching out side of water is like pressing through your in-between place with your own mind set to do it the way you want to, the way that you have decided is best for you. Now deciding to be stretched in the water is like allowing the Holy Spirit of God to instruct you by speaking to your mind on what to do, how to do, and when to do. Your ability to prayerfully submit yourself and relax in the spirit of God will cause the stretching that you must go through to get you through your in-between place to be easier. This stretching has been designed just for you and it has been designed in such a way that you will find that Jesus, because of your obedience to submit and allow him to be in control, has already spoke to the winds of your in-between place and said "Peace Be Still". This makes clear the scripture in Isaiah 54:17 which says, "No weapon that is formed against thee shall proper…" although there are winds designed in your in-between place to knock you off course it will accomplish what the enemy has designed it to do. It is when you are able to recognize the process is designed to bring forth the will of God in you and it is not a natural war but a spiritual, you will be able to hold on. Listen again to the word of God that may be able to help you get through if you will allow it. II Corinthians 10:4-5 says, "For the weapons of our warfare are not carnal, but mighty through God to the pulling down of strongholds; casting down imaginations, and every high thing that exalteth itself against the knowledge of God, and bringing into captivity every thought to the obedience of Christ."

Hopefully you can step back and take another look, not through your natural eyes, but through the eyes of God and see that this process and this in-between place is spiritual and it is about your willingness to allow your mind to settle and become obedient to Christ. Allow this process to have full effect in your life and begin to see yourself moving across to the other side. The process is to get you to the other side of everything that the enemy has designed to hold you back. The Lord only want what is good for you and it is up to you to stretch pass the old and see what is right before you as you go through this place called in-between. Philippians 2:13 says, "For it is God which worketh in you both to will and to do of his good pleasure." It pleases God to bring you through any and every place that you have difficulty crossing, that you may arrive at the position he has already prepared just for you. Take the time to recognize that everything you need to succeed in Christ is already prepared for you. God is not trying to get things ready for you, to help you through; it is already ready and was prepared for you from the beginning of time. Stop trying to figure God out, just submit to his will for your life, and sweetly follow his spirit as it leads you.

Grace

We are able to get through our process because the grace of God is there with us to freely help us get through. Jesus' response to Apostle Paul in, what I would like to call, one of his in-between places was "My grace is sufficient for thee: for my strength is made perfect in weakness" (II Corinthians 12:9). It is God's grace that takes us through our in-between places, and helps us to be able to recognize that nothing and no one can sustain us, sustain our mind or our inner most being, in the middle of all that we may be encountering, nothing but the grace of God.

When you are able to recognize what grace has already done, then, you will be able to face every in-between place with peace. It is realizing that whatever the price may have been to get you through that in-between place, it has already been paid because God's grace truly is sufficient. This is the encouragement that will help you to move into a peaceful frame of mind, knowing that the grace of God is in place to help you go through your in-between place. Your process is designed just for you and it is necessary to get you exactly where you should be because of your destiny.

Why is it that people fear process, have you given it any

thought? Process is something that you can't avoid because in one-way or another every person go through some form of process, whether they realize it or not. If you were able to see in advance the process that you were facing, as one of the things that has been designed to get you through this place called in-between, you would eventually become thankful, because it will work for your good.

Learn how to become prayerful for your process and allow it to take you into a smooth transition as you go through your in-between place. Everything that you don't understand does not always work against you, but it can bring you into a place of seeking God more. Not understanding something will cause you, hopefully, to seek understanding, therefore, it will cause you to draw close to God through prayer for the understanding that you need and seek.

The Ability to Discern Jesus

God's love is there for people that will accept that love and trust it to sustain them in every weak and doubting area in their lives. When you are in the middle of what seem like the greatest storm of your life, if you will just blindly hold on to the promise of God, to never leave you nor forsake you, you will find that his love is very sustaining. To know that the risen savior is right there holding you up so that you will not sink, it will give you hope to continue trusting, not in what you can see or what you can make sense of but trusting in what he has promised.

When learning to trust in what you can't see or understand, it's your faith that will carry you through your in-between places. Faith is not based on what you can see or understand, you may not even like the way things are going, but you yet must trust in the Lord with all your heart and continue to remind yourself, God can't lie therefore he must fulfill his every promise to me. It is important that every person remind themselves that, God is not an everyday Santa that is there to give you your every, whelm. He is the keeper of your soul (mind, will, and emotions), there to do what is best for you and to bring you into that perfect place, to allow his plan for your future to be fulfilled. Continue to remember that there will be times when you are uncomfortable with the situation but he is working that situation out for your good.

God's plan for you is for your good and not for evil. Jesus came that you might have peace, he is the author of peace therefore, relax and trust him to do what he does best and that is to bring you to an expected end, His, not yours. Learn how to commit your way to God's way and know that he won't let you down with the trust you place in him.

Life will constantly present you with obstacles and this is a form of an in-between place but you must learn how to be able to discern the voice of God in these places. Some years ago there was a saying "what would Jesus do?" and many were wearing bracelets with "WWJD" on them. It became a fad but I often wondered how many of those people wearing the sign on their body really acknowledged the Lord in every decision they made before they made it, to see what he would do in their particular situations. Did they not only acknowledge him in each decision but also wait for an answer from him. Did they wait and try to discern what would be pleasing to their savior, be it through the move of his spirit or something given through His written word (the bible).

If you ask for Jesus' help, he will give you help. He gives assurances to his people through his spirit and his word. Through his spirit when there is a calmness that comes upon you and maybe a thought that may come to your mind that you just feel lead to do something, by faith just trust that leading and do it. The people of old times use to have a saying "if it's God it will work, if it is not it won't". Don't be ashamed if you feel that the Lord has given you something to do and you act on that leading and later find that it did not work out, just simply say that you thought it was God. Never be afraid to trust those urges again, this is how you will be able to learn to discern the voice of Jesus.

Next, is to be able to discern the voice of God through his word. As you seek his help, you should find scriptures that will give you the assurance that his word is there for your help, scriptures like Proverbs 3:6 which says "In all thy ways acknowledge him, and he shall direct thy paths." God's word assures you, if you will consult him first, he will direct you in which way to go or tell you what you should do. Now you have two choices, seek him by his spirit or through his word. When you are learning how to discern God's voice also learn to be patient and to have faith, it takes both.

There was a time when I felt so unsure of discerning the Lord's voice that I constantly would say to him, "help me Lord, I need help." I would acknowledge him in this way day and night. It did not matter what I was doing my first reaction was the same "help me Lord, I need help". I had gotten to the point that while I slept I would wake up out of a sound sleep, sit up in bed and say "help me Lord, I need help" then, lay down again and go back to sleep. Even when I didn't realize it I was acknowledging my savior for his direction in my life with every decision. When you ask for direction he will give you direction.

In that same chapter of Proverbs it tells you not to lean to your own understanding but trust him (v.5). You may second-guess yourself but you never have to worry about second-guessing the Lord. It's good to know that you have someone that you can go to that will never lie to you, someone that always has your best interest at heart and will always tell you what is best for you, that will always work for your good. What a mighty God we serve, a God that loves each of us equally even when we didn't love ourselves.

The in-between place can have some very rough days; then again there can be days of peace as you go through that day. Just like the waves of the sea, the disciples were on waves that were some times higher as the waves blew but when the wind subsided those same waves calmed. It is in our ability to cope with the winds and the waves that come in our in-between that will take us to the next test that will surly come. It is how you feel about this place called in-between that will determine how you get through it. Will you be like the disciples that ran to Jesus in the middle of the storm and said "master carest thou not that we perish?" It is really amazing how the Lord's children, in the middle of their storms will run to the master (Jesus) to question His love and concern for his people. Did he not say to us "…I have loved thee with an everlasting love…" the love and the care that the Father has for us, there is no end but will you love him enough to trust his care and concern for you.

Make up your mind that although I'm in an in-between place right now I'm going to stand up and get myself through this place. I will allow God to use this place to make me what I need to be to get through the plan He has for me. I will walk out this process of completing God's plan that has been designed just for me. This is not a day of your captivity you are free in Christ Jesus. St. John 8:3 says "If the Son therefore shall make you free, ye shall be free indeed" then Galatians 5:1 tells you to "stand fast therefore in the liberty wherewith Christ hath made us free, and be not entangled again with the yoke of bondage." You are no longer prisoners to sin or to people. Jesus is taking you somewhere; prepare to follow, through humble submission.

Learn how to humble yourself and let the Lord transition you. You can't get to the place you need to be until you are able to discern the voice of God that tells you when to stand still and hear his will. Listen! Jesus is speaking. He wants to speak into your spirit the instructions that you will need to be transitioned. There were words to a song once that said "hush, hush, somebody's calling my name. Hush, hush, somebody's calling my name, oh it must be the voice of the

Lord." I'm not sure those are the exact words but I do know that if we would quite ourselves we would be able to hear the master calling our name to come up to a place of transition. Maybe you should take the time and ask the master if he is calling your name. Just ask him, Jesus, are you calling my name? Don't be afraid to ask, if you ask it means you are willing to hear. If the master is calling for you something good may be about to happen in your life, transition.

There was a blind man whom the scripture called Bartimeus, he was a bagger but when he heard that Jesus was coming by his way, began to call out to Jesus and although the people tried to quite him he did not allow them to stop him because he was able, even in a darken place, to discern the healing power of Jesus. Bartimeus' ability to discern that Jesus was near caused Jesus to discern the cry of Bartimeus in his midst and Jesus stood still and commanded that Bartimeus be called. Therefore, the people said to Bartimeus "Be of good comfort, rise; he calleth thee." (Mark 11:49. If you will get in the position to discern Jesus, Jesus will discern you and your need and he will call you by your name. Also Mary, the sister of Lazarus, in her time of sorrow needed something that could not be given to her by others but Jesus called her by name, because Martha said to Mary secretly, the master is come and calleth for thee. Whenever you are able to discern the master, who he is in your midst you will find that he has already discerned you a long time ago and he will call you by your name to do for you what you can't do for yourself. Jesus wants to transition you.

Discernment is important to those seeking something from the Lord because you can't get that which is holy from that which is unholy. There is no strength in that which is weak. If you need life you don't go to someone that is dead. Jesus, the life giver wants to give you life that you never be the same again. Jesus says "…I am come that they might have life, and that they might have it more abundantly, John 10:10." The abundant life that Jesus gives, will give you the ability to discern Jesus, the one that gives you, life.

The ability to discern Jesus, the voice of God, the strength of God, and even the courage of God, will help to sustain you in any situation you find yourself in. That ability helps you to separate your doubt and fears from your trust and faith in the Lord. Jesus says, "my sheep hear my voice, and I know them, and they follow me" John 10:27. Therefore you follow who you know because you have the ability to discern who Jesus is.

Please understand that this ability to discern Jesus comes through spending time with him in prayer and reading the scriptures. Take time to meditate on his word, allowing him opportunity to speak into your spirit learn how to hunger for the more of Jesus and not to let your days slip away from you without spending time with him. The closer you draw to him the closer he will be to you, allowing you the experience of discerning the Lord's presence as well as the ability to discern the voice of the Lord. These things should not become a task but a pleasure.

If you hunger for the more of him and if you thirst for him, his word will be fulfilled in you. What do you truly want the Lord to do for you and in you? Think about that then set yourself goals then work toward those goals. Ask God to help you be able to discern him the more with true sensitivity to his spirit and his will in your life. Be blessed as you grow in your new relationship of discernment with Jesus.

Day Star Arise

Today is a day of divine peace, a day that God is doing something in my heart. This is a day of sunshine both in and out. It is a beautiful, sunny day outside but truly within my heart the sunshine of the Lord is shining bright. II Peter 1:19 says "we have also a more sure word of prophecy; where unto ye do well that ye take heed, as unto a light that shineth in a dark place, until the day dawn and the day star arise in your heart." The day star can arise in your life through the peace of God, that peace which comes through your faith in Jesus Christ, a peace that is not found in the world. Jesus said "Peace I leave with you, my peace I give unto you: not as the world giveth, give I unto you…"
(John 14:27). Don't try to imagine this peace that Jesus will give as the kind you search for in the world for the peace Jesus offers is far beyond that. This is why the sun is able to shine in your heart as well as all around you although it could be a cloudy day on the outside. The storms of life may be rocking your ship but there can be such a calm in your spirit, because the peace of Jesus has been given to you through your faith, and it has cause the day star to arise in you.

This is a good time to trust God and exercise your faith to allow the day star to arise in your marriage, your children, siblings or even that relationship that has seemed hopeless for a long time, the day star is able to arise right now to allow the sunshine of peace and joy to manifest itself to you. Stop trying to figure this out just put your trust in a God that does not fail and can't lie (Deut. 31:6, Num. 23:19).

Take a moment to think about what areas of your life you need the peace of God in, where do you need the sun to shine? Don't be afraid to trust. It is not about the trust as much as it is about who or what you trust. When you feel the warmth of that day star when it arise you become relaxed and feel that peace. Not only will you be able to feel that peace but you will, through the spirit, have been bathed in the oil of joy and dressed in the garment of praise. Hallelujah, give God praise for He is worthy.

Now is a good time to allow God to do a new thing in you. It is a promise of God for he has said, "Behold, I will do a new thing; now it shall spring forth; shall ye not know it? I will even make a way in the wilderness, and rivers in the desert" (Isaiah 43:19). When he said, "I will", then you will have to allow him to do what he wants to do in you. Allow him to do for you what has never been done before. If it is going to be a "new thing" that would mean it has never been done before. The day star is able to arise in your dry places and give you something that you have needed for a long time, that something that will make you compete in Him.

Stars bring such brightness into a dark place. It does not matter how dark your night season may be, a star can be seen billons of miles away, and how powerful that is. Jesus is our bright and morning star, there shining out in the sin covered life but even the blackness of sin can't hold back the light of Christ. Whatever the situation may be allow Christ to arise in that situation. If you will exercise the faith you can receive a miracle this very moment.

The joy of the Lord is what you need right now in your life; it will launch you forward in the things of God. You can have such a move of God that you won't be able to comprehend it all but you will be able to feel the brightness of the day star shining from within you, making things new and bright. It will be like looking through new eyes and all will see the inner glow that will spring forth. The day star can and will arise just for you, in you. It too will be like launching a rocket for all the world to see and the day and the time is based on you, are you ready, just say yes.

Jesus spoke a word into his disciples about his being transfigured and his clothing began to shine or glow like nothing they had ever seen before and Moses and Elijah came and talked with Jesus (Dead men walking, Praise God), Mark 9:2-3. Then Jesus spoke into his followers and others looking on concerning a man's son, "If thou canst believe, all things are possible to him that believeth" (V. 23). If you will just trust Jesus you will not only be able to see but you will be able to experience the day star of the Holy Ghost arise and shine out in you and your life. Remember that Jesus said "If" thou canst believe. Do you believe Jesus today can command the day star to rise up in your life and shine forth that you may know that he abides within you? This is not about what others believe, but if you can believe, all things are possible to you. As you reflect on this day star I pray that the Holy Spirit will give you understanding and there be an unfolding for you in the spirit. With this day star you can have the very presence of the Lord in you shining bright for all to see. Jesus said that He is the bright and morning star, (Rev. 22:16). He was giving the hearers a sure word of prophecy but only those with spiritual ears would be able to truly hear what Jesus was saying. This is the same truth of the day star, it is there for those that has a sensitive ear to the spirit of God. There are some things that we may not fully understand but it is up to each of us to trust God to give revelation knowledge enough to yield to his spirit and allow the spirit to have its way in us. The day star when it arise in your life will work within you too reach the world for Christ, it is part of God's fulfillment for you and in you. Now can you with a true heart say, Day Star Arise, because you are able to discern Jesus wanting to do more for you, listen he want to arise in you.

Looking in the Mirror

Your in-between place can be a place of much difficulty, when you find yourself in uncomfortable or difficult situation don't fear, doubt or fret. If you don't know what to do or who to trust, pray. Jesus said, "pray without ceasing", he also said "men ought always to pray and not faint." He did not stop there but he continued to give assurance by saying "Be careful (anxious) for nothing but in everything with prayer and thanksgiving let your request be made known unto God" (I Thess. 5:17; Luke 18:1; Phil. 4:6). Jesus took the time throughout the scriptures to encourage his people to pray. If you submit your request to him he is there waiting to answer.

In my last book "A Healing Within" there was a brief writing on the killings at Fort Hood, to my surprise at the writing of this book there has been another killing at Fort Hood. There are people that can't handle the pressures that come sometime in an in-between place. The wars that you battle many times are in the mind. When people are fighting wars in their mind, having to make decisions and don't know what to do, they find themselves, many times, making the wrong decision, the decision that take the lives of others as well many times their own life. It is the wars of the mind and the emotions that many times catch others unaware.

Where do you go, what do you do, when you find yourself in

an in-between place fighting a war that you are unsure how to win? A war not only of the mind or a war that has your emotions out of control but even that giant war of fear, what do you do? The word of the Lord tells us "God is our refuge and strength, a very present help in trouble" (Ps. 46:1). When you are weak the Lord is your strength and when trouble come, he is your help. He says, "Be still and know that I am God" (vs.10). Learn how to trust the Lord at his word. Just as Jesus' disciples ran to the hinder part of the ship to seek out Jesus when the storm came and the spirit of fear gripped them, that same Jesus is with you riding out the storms that may come in your in-between place. Don't allow fear to make you think that Jesus, your savior, is not with you or that he don't care about you or what happens to you.

Don't become anxious at the adversary's words, stand still and truly know that God is God in or out of an in-between place. The battle is not yours; it's the Lord's (I Sam. 17:47). Jesus don't need your help to fight his battle he has taken victory over every battle a long time ago. Learn how to conquer the doubts that may come in your in-between place and allow yourself to be strengthened so you may grow in the power and the anointing of the Lord.

God is an on time God, he is never too early nor is he ever too late because he is, "Alpha and Omega, the beginning and the ending..." (Rev. 1:8). When anyone need him he is there.

Things come our way in this in-between place to help us know if we truly trust him. Every person has to keep the word of God in their heart, continue to remember what he has promised each of his people "...I will never leave thee, nor forsake thee" (Deut. 31:6, 8; Heb. 13:5). You must remember the Lord is with you working what is perfect in him to bring his people to perfection doing what is right. It is to teach his people to trust what he is doing in them. Don't allow yourself to forget that whatever is happening in this in-between place of yours is happening for your good.

In Deuteronomy 8:2 God began to explain to his children that those things he allowed to come upon them were for their good. He said to them "And thou shalt remember all the way which the Lord thy God led thee these forty years in the wilderness to humble thee, and to prove thee to know what was in thine heart, whether thou wouldest keep his commandments or no". Just listen to what God had to say to his children, he call them to remember and to know what was in their hearts. Can't you see the need to check yourself in your in-between place? Don't allow what happens in the in-between place to make you doubt God. Know what is in your heart. Therefore when storms arise in your life or any of our lives it is the Lord pushing each of us to take a look in the mirror and see what is there, will you obey his word or no. Now get to the place that you desire to be, close to him, not because you fear the storm but because you long to be close to him, being transformed to be more like him. This is about you not someone else and it is time to know the real war. Where does it come from, how did I get here and how do I get out? You must learn what this is truly all about if you even intend to be free. One important thing you must keep in mind is to be free you must go through your in-between place because; it is your only way out.

You are encouraged through instructions how to get and stay ready; you should "Put on the whole armor of God, that ye may be able to stand against the wiles (schemes) of the devil" (Eph. 6:11). The ability to face truth will help you get to the place you need to be in order to survive the journey. If you face the real truth of your life and follow the instructions laid out to you through much of the scripture you will be able to make it. The Scripture (the word of God) is important to every person no matter what the situation if you will trust it. To do this you must, many times, take a good look in the mirror.

I must remind you that every person will have to face their place called in-between. This is a place that is different for each individual because it is based on their individual self. What they face and how they may encounter the task of getting through to the plan Christ has for their life is based many times on their obedience to the word of God.

As I prayed on the in-between place, it became very clear to me why we struggle. The hardship does not come with getting through this place but rather facing the truths that we must learn to be transparent with as we go through. Truths about ourselves, who we really are, our weaknesses and our strengths. Our fears, the fears that causes us to shy away from looking in the mirror of our realities. The realities that you don't really want to face, those that you pretend are not there. This is the true war of our in-between place. Yes, this place called in-between can be a war but what you must realize is the war is with yourself not with things, nor with others. Just think of those things you have been suppressing for years, things you have prayed that no one would ever find out about, but you fight with your own mind on a regular bases trying hard not to face your real truths. This is the war, your war of your in-between place. These real truths are the winds that are blowing so fierce against your spiritual ship and the waves that are beating so high and hard against your soul. Let today be the day that you say to your soul "no more" I acknowledge the master that is in the ship with me and through him I can declare peace. I can command the winds and the waves of my mind to be still in the name of Jesus because through His name I can do all things. It is in and through Jesus that you can be sure that you will make it through your in-between place to the other side.

Now look in the mirror, and acknowledge the release of every obstacle that has been holding you back. Those things that had been beating like waves against your ship and those things that were the spiritual winds blowing against your mind. Acknowledge them null and void in your life, released from your soul. Speak to yourself; tell yourself that you are free. Be reminded of I Samuel 16:7 and just as God encouraged Samuel, you too can be reminded and encouraged by the word of God "…the Lord seeth not as man seeth; for man looketh on the outward appearance, but the Lord looketh on the heart". By this you should be encouraged just to know that God sees your heart and when you look in the mirror look pass what the natural eye see and look deep in to the truth of your own heart and see the release of all the old and see the true joy and peace of the new you. Be blessed, in the field, be blessed in the city, be thou blessed upon the waters that your spiritual ship sails upon. Therefore hold your head up and let the King of Glory come in and shine in your heart.

Every step you take by faith will take you to a deeper place in your walk of faith in the Lord. If you will stand in faith every expectation you have in the Lord according to his will shall be accomplished. Don't allow people or things to take from you what you have fought for in the spirit. The master declares peace in your in-between place and you must go to the other side because he has a plan for your life and it must and will be accomplished. Allow yourself to take a good look into that perfect law of liberty that you be a doer of the things you have been instructed to do that you be and continue to be blessed (James 1:25). It is that perfect law of liberty that has become the mirror that you and every believer must look into if you truly want to be free. Don't willingly jump ship in your in-between place just because a storm come. Be thankful for the storms that come to help push you to the other side and say like the psalmist "I shall not die, but live and declare the works of the Lord" (Ps. 118:17). It's time to live, therefore take a good look into the mirror, what is looking back at you? There are times when individuals see what they want to see when they take a look in the mirror. But, it is not about what you want to see or even what you choose to see, when you look in the mirror through the eyes of the Lord based on his word and praying for His spirit to show you truth, you will see truth. Jesus told his disciples "And ye shall know the truth, and the truth shall make you free" (John 8:32). It is that truth in the word of God that will help you see the real person in the mirror.

Trusting the Lord to show you yourself through his spirit will help to face what it is that you will see looking at you in that mirror. When is the last time that you ask God how does he see you? Did you wait on God to give you the answer and if so, did you like the answer that you received. There are times that I have not always liked the answers I have received from the Lord but through tears I asked for forgiveness, then I ask the Lord to help me. It is up to you to decide if what you are seeing, when you look in the mirror, is true, your truth or God's and what are you going to do about it. Your life in Christ is affected by what you see and what you do when you look in that spiritual mirror. Don't attempt to change truth but humble yourself and allow truth to change you. Keep in mind that this is spiritual but it can and will have a profound effect in your life if you will let it. Jesus said, "I am the way, the truth, and the life…" (John 14:6).

Give some thought to why people look in the mirror. It is to see if there are flaws, to see if everything is in place or if something you don't want others to see is showing. There are also times when you visit the mirror to see how good something look by some changes that has been made. The point is regardless to what you might see when you look in the mirror, allow Christ to show you what is true and to bring change to anything that will bring out the best in you and those things that will give him the glory. Looking in the mirror will keep you moving forward in Christ, especially when you are looking to see what Christ want you to see. I Corinthians 13 says "…Now we see through a glass (mirror), darkly; but then face-to-face…but then shall I know even as also I am known" (vs.12).

There are times we really don't see things as they truly are, although we are looking and searching for truth. But Christ has come to do away with those things that we see in part, causing us to see them dimly because we don't see the full picture that is right before us. It is through Christ that we are able to boldly look into that perfect law (mirror) of liberty, which will help each of us to see things within ourselves as they truly are.

Looking in the mirror that is before you will help you know how to pray and what you should be praying about. It is difficult to see defects and not desire corrections to be made. Therefore as we are looking into the Holy Ghost mirror that is before each of us we should desire better. David was reminded of the things that he thought was behind him and when he looked in the mirror his cry to the Lord was "create in me a clean heart, O God; and renew a right spirit within me. Cast me not away from thy presence" (Psalm 51:10-11a). God through the prophet Nathan was the mirror that reminded David of what was right before him. God through his spirit will be the mirror that will help you see what you need to see. The things that God is not pleased with will be there in your mirror looking back at you when you choose to look in that mirror. Don't turn and run away from the things you see but cry out to the Lord just as David did. He cried out desiring to come into a right standing with the Lord. In Psalm 51:6

David had to acknowledge that God "desirest truth in the inward parts". The mirror that you look into will show you what is in your inward parts. If you see something that is not the desires of the Lord, something that does not give him glory, be humble enough to acknowledge it and repent to the Lord and you just might need to repent to others also. In verse 3 of this same psalms David said, "my sin is ever before me", you see the mirror won't let you get by if you truly desire the truth in your inward parts.

David was considered a man after God's own heart, but he had some issues and so do we. Jesus' teaching on the mount declared "they which do hunger and thirst after righteousness shall be filled" (Matthew 5:6). If the desire is in you to do what is right and to know what is within you, you have a savior that will not only allow you to see where you are but he will also forgive when you repent out of a sincere heart and he alone is able to eradicate every sin and every weakness that has had you held up in your spirit from being free in Christ.

Take the time to press toward that higher calling in Christ Jesus. This calling will help you to press forward to get through that in-between place as you look in the mirror of the things that you bound. Thanks be to God that give you the victory. He is the God that is willing to help believers that loves him, to deal with their issues. You may feel like you are not a believer but if you believe in Jesus, believe that he died for your sins, deliverance is yours. You first must understand that Jesus love you whether you love him or not. He died for you whether you accept it or not. These are the issues that many have in their life and they don't know how to handle their issues but just say yes to the love and the help that he is offering. It takes pressing but be assured that Jesus is there to help you press and if you are willing to press, there is a prize awaiting you. This should help you to know how to handle what you see in the mirror.

Facing Your Brokenness

The place known as in-between can be a painful place but also a place of healing. It is a place to recognize your brokenness and face up to it. Brokenness is something that many times a person does not want to face up to because of the pain that it entails as well as admitting that there is some brokenness. Because a person does not admit to the brokenness doesn't mean the pain is not there.

Brokenness comes from a lot of suppressing those things you don't want to face. Things that you are not willing to admit to yourself that they even exist. The many painful things that you don't have answers to or you don't know where to find the answers. Suppression comes with that inability to begin taking inventory of the things you don't know how to handle at the present time.

It is not just the in-between place or the brokenness that you face in the place but part of it is what conditions you to get through your in-between place and into the future that God has planned for you. No one wants to hurt or struggle, it is the pain that causes a person to withdraw to a place of brokenness and not want to look at the path that is designed to strengthen them as they are being conditioned for their future. Looking at your present condition will cause a delay in what God want to do in your life for you. You can't move forward if you become stuck on where you are, being stuck is the thing that causes your brokenness too began. When you allow yourself to become stuck you can't go back and you can't move forward, but God wants his people to move forward. It was never God's will for the children of Israel to become stuck in the wilderness but to move forward to the Promised Land.

To get to the Promised Land the children of Israel had to learn process. Every child of the Most High God and follower of the Lord Jesus Christ must learn how to get through the process by following God's instructions step by step. This mean to read his word, meditate on it and apply it every day in your life. It is your love for the Lord that will drive you to apply the process. When the process is applied it will help you to move forward. Forward to the next step in the process. Your process will help you to see things in a new light, things are not always the way it appears to the natural eye. Your process will help you to see things through the eyes of God (spiritually). When what you view is flawed, then it is broken. Brokenness causes a person to not be in working order, they become weaken, not complete. It is in these conditions that you must be able to know what steps to apply, steps such as, acknowledging the Lord in all your ways and believing that he will direct your paths, (Prov.3:6).

There is something that every child of God must keep in

mind, just know that no matter how many times you use a scripture, you may need that same scripture over and over again, if it is what will get you through your process and strengthen you in your brokenness, use it. It is not about how many different scriptures you can quote, but which part of God's word will help strengthen your broken place or places. The word of God is important, every word, you must keep yourself reminded of this. Scriptures such as "thy word have I hid in mine heart, that I might not sin against thee", or "I will not forget thy word" (Psalm 119:11,1b). When a child of God refuse to acknowledge God's word or keep it afresh in their mind, and heart, you may become flawed.

When you walk in brokenness and you're unsure how to face that brokenness it is very important to be able to reflect on the word of God and know that His word will bring you into a place in Him that will strengthen you and make you whole again, if you are willing to trust the process of His word.

There are times a person has to face what they don't want to face and acknowledge what they don't want to acknowledge for the weak places to be made strong and the broken places to be mended.

Facing your brokenness means you have to face the fact that the waves in your life is raging and the winds are blowing. Facing your brokenness means that you have a fear and a feeling of helplessness. It is only when you acknowledge that you are not alone and you can reflect back on the promises of God, promises such as "I will never leave thee, nor forsake thee" (Deut. 31:6, 8; Heb.13:5), that you can look on your brokenness with hope that your heavenly father is with you and will see you through your process and help you back to wholeness again.

It is not so much the brokenness that is a problem but, the facing of your brokenness. It is necessary to be able to be transparent when dealing with your broken places. The ability to acknowledge that there is some form of brokenness in your life and be able to identify what and where those broken places are in your life is very important. There are times that an individual is able to say they may have some form of brokenness but from that point they want to move on, they don't want to stop and visit the broken places because the pain is too great. This is why one must be able to face the brokenness, address the pain and the areas you are weak in or you won't be able to effectively move forward. Moving forward is more than simply saying you want to move forward, you must be willing to do the work of moving forward.

Self-Exam

This is an area that has made me take another look at myself.

I've had to examine myself and recognize that I have a lot of brokenness within me that I had not realized before this chapter of the book when God moved upon me to search myself and acknowledge that, even now I'm walking in some broken places. Places that I have not been willing to see, because of the pain of really taking a good look at some of the ways that I'm affected by everyday life, is greater than I wanted to deal with. Our everyday life has a great effect on our in-between place. If an individual is unwilling to face or seek out what it is that is causing them to effectively move forward then, they become stagnant and unable to move from their in-between place thus, causing them to sink in their in-between place fighting unsuccessfully their own brokenness. So I struggle, but I'm fighting to ensure that I don't sink in my struggle and succumb to my brokenness. Yes, I used the word, my. Until I am able to acknowledge what is going on I won't be able to conquer it. Except with the Lord's help and his strength that he gives me when I'm weak. You must be able to admit what is happening to you, that you be able to overcome it. For when I'm weak (broken) then in Him am I made strong.

Walls of deceit has caused me some brokenness. Unreciprocated love and pretense has caused me to be broken and began to withdraw into a place of seclusion within myself. It is these types of things that start the brokenness but there are many other things that causes the broken places to increase. Therefore, rather than just lay down and die we become busy with other things. Things like praying with others that they may overcome, and searching the scriptures to be able to teach others how to trust God, that He will see them through their troubled times staying in prayer that his will be done. All the while not acknowledging our own hurts and our own brokenness. After a while you don't even see yourself as broken because you have used every resource to suppress the facts so that you don't have to look at them but you can't suppress the pain.

After a while you don't even know why you are feeling the pain. It don't always surface but it does surface periodically so you just pray and keep it moving. Acknowledge it or not the fact is we're broken and the brokenness is working to destroy the person God want each of us to be. It is important that we examine ourselves taking a truly good look at what is going on within us that we too can be healed. Facing the brokenness is about being healed. We face it so that we can truly acknowledge it, allowing God to kill the root of this brokenness and take it out of us cleansing our soul (our mind, will, and emotions). There must be a willingness to truly face some of our greatest pain in order that we be healed.

The willingness to confront yourself in your brokenness also allows the spirit of God, which is the Holy Ghost or Holy

Spirit to reveal to you the things in your life that you feel are alright. But it is in the eyes of God that truly see you in bondage and it is causing you to become more broken than you realize. Your brokenness is a form of bondage and it will hold you back from becoming truly free in Christ Jesus. Please recognize that the things that hold you in a state of brokenness is because you have kept Jesus out by thinking that you can handle things on your own and not seeing the toll things are having on you and your spiritual freedom as well as your spiritual growth. Therefore, the Lord is unable to set you free from your brokenness. Remember that Jesus will not over ride your will to let him in to work His will in you. He is standing at the door of your heart knocking but, you must let him in and give him complete freedom to work. His word says "If the Son therefore shall make you free, ye shall be free indeed" (John 8:36). The chains of your brokenness can be broken and you can be free (delivered) from your brokenness. At this time in the life of the children and servants of the Most High there is no room to be hindered from fulfilling the charge given to you from the Lord. It was not given to you to stay in your in-between place broken, unsure, and somewhat afraid. It is necessary to cross to the other side that His plan for your life be accomplished. Your future is before you and the weight of your brokenness is not a part of your God planned future. The Apostle Paul wrote, "But I keep under my body, and bring it into subjection: lest that by any means, when I have preached to others, I myself should be a castaway" (I Cor. 9:27).

There has been so much brokenness within me that it stagnated the ministry and mission given to me by the Lord. The thing is, I didn't even realize it. You may say, how did I not realize it? I was too busy preaching to others, helping them get delivered that I didn't know what was causing my own pain. Facing it has been the greatest task of all. Believe me when I say to you that you can get true deliverance and move forward, I know this through experience.

Right now in this season of your life allow yourself to believe that there is a God that can and will heal you and truly deliver you, once and for all. A God that is willing to restore back unto you all that was taken. The brokenness that we each share in some form or another, we can be proclaimed as healed, and then be totally free to move forward, not looking back.

Whatever caused the brokenness in your life it is necessary to forgive that thing quickly and keep it moving forward. The same way that we wanted God to forgive us, that is the same way we must forgive others. The Lord let me know to forgive quickly and keep it moving. I must truly (from my heart), forgive quickly and keep it moving, for it is what the Lord did for me and this time all things will be different. Precious people of God don't look back, be free from the brokenness that has you bound. If you will believe with all that is in you, in all that you know how to believe, trusting God, then, you are free and you are whole. Now that you are stronger, you can feel yourself becoming happier than you were before and your spiritual bones are mending. Put on your garment of praise and allow the oil of Joy to overflow in your life. You are moving forward because the plan of God for your future is waiting and you must through faith and obedience, to the master, cross over to the other side. Leave those things that were released in your in-between place, leave it, and there is no room for it in the place Jesus is taking you.

I'm reminded of the lepers that said, "Why sit we here until we die" (II Kings 7:3). Precious people you must get up and seek out the instructions of God in this your in-between place of brokenness for God is speaking. Remember there is no room for brokenness where he is taking you, but these instructions that he is giving, you must be able to hear and understand that you may do. There may be times when you become torn wanting to hear a word from the Lord, you may seek him in an everyday search, seeking to know what Jesus has to say but it seems as though you can't hear what he is saying.

There have been times that I have thought, I'm seeking a word from you Lord but I don't hear what you are saying. You may recognize that I said, I don't hear, what God is saying to me, some time. Have you ever felt this way? Seeking answers from God but you don't hear him. Stop and get this picture clear, I don't hear, not I can't hear. God is speaking to each of us in so many different ways but because we expect the answer in a certain way and at a certain time, we don't hear him. You would be able to hear if you would allow yourself to move out from that place of brokenness, recognizing it is a process and you don't have to stay there, you can began to step out in faith, and truly long to hear God in any way that he choose to speak. Then, that small still voice that you will be able to hear will become clear.

When God is speaking you must be truly willing to hear the answers that he is giving. Now began learning how to listen, he will teach you how to hear his voice. Every night my prayer is "I need you to speak to me and allow me to hear and understand what you are saying to me." Give me the strength to be obedient Lord, to what you say unto me. Even when I can understand what God speaks I continue with that same form of prayer, why? Because I want and need an open communication type relationship with my savior.

Do you hear God when he speaks to you? Are you seeking answers and it seems like there are none? Do you have an open two-way communication with the Father or is it a one-way talk. Isaiah says "Seek ye the Lord while he may be found, call ye upon him while he is near," (55:6). If you and I continue to seek God to speak, with expectation, we will began to hear him in his timing. Patience is very important in seeking God and his answers and I'm here to tell you he will answer. While you're seeking your answers from the Lord remember that you don't have to strain to hear him. He is right there with you and he has been there all the time, he has been waiting for you to realize that he is there.

God does not want any of his children to feel lonely and broken but, that is the feeling that comes when your relationship with the Father has been hindered. If you are unable to truly communicate with the one that has died and shed his blood for you, then you have a broken relationship, one that is lonely without the savior. While you seek answers you just might find that your answers from the Lord may be "my grace is sufficient for thee…" (II Cor. 12:9). The solution you need for every situation is covered by God's grace. Therefore, whatever answer you seek just know that when it come, it comes wrapped in grace.

There is a season of brokenness that will make the answers to your unanswered questions seem as though they are far away but continue to pursue the Lord for your answer and know that he is speaking. This may be a part of your season of brokenness and you may be searching, but go through your process and step-by-step you will get your answers. Your communication with the Lord will become clear and your brokenness will be healed. This in-between place of brokenness is only a season, face it, it is a part of the process of an in-between place that will help your spiritual ears to become sensitive to hearing the spirit of the Lord that step by step you will walk it out and be healed. Wrapped in your garment of praise the pain will no longer have the same power over you and God will get the glory. Jesus is inviting you to go to the other side of your brokenness where there is joy, hear, obey and be healed because the master cares for you.

By Faith Follow

When you are in your in-between place it is a place you are standing by faith. It is the place where you don't know what lay before you and it's too rocky and too dark to look back to the things that are behind you. This is the place that you should be willing to stand right where you are, knowing that the God you serve is well able to keep you from falling. Jude 24-25 has been used throughout Christendom as a benediction but let me give you another view of this same scripture. When you are in a place, let's say your "in-between place", you don't know what is ahead and you dare not go back to the old place. It is at this time that you will have to decide if you will trust your savior or sink in your storm, it is then you can reflect on the master and say, "Now unto Him that is able to keep ME from falling". You have to know for yourself that Jesus is well able to take you to the place that he (Jesus) has ask you to go, the other side. If he said "let us cross to the other side" that is where you will end up if you will just trust him to take you there.

Precious people of God you don't always have to know every step, all the directions, or how long it will take to get there but just trust the one that is taking you there, Jesus. Whether he is asleep (you think), or awake keep in mind that you are sailing with a savior that can't lie therefore you will arrive at the destination that he has set for you, alive. According to Matthew 9:29 Jesus' word to his followers is "According to your faith be it unto you…" therefore you sweetly, humbly, follow by faith. The in-between place can be a difficult place if you can't use your faith to follow. It is in your in-between place that you don't have all the answers and this is why your mustard seed faith is important. It does not take a lot of faith but the smallest amount will take you to places you never dreamed you could go.

By faith follow the one that is well able to fulfill every promise and remove every fear. It is by faith that you follow even though the tears want to fall and by faith follow when it seems as though you are hoping against hope. Every person must follow by faith because it is not your plan that has been set into motion, but God's plan through Jesus designed just for you. By faith follow, through pain, heartache, sickness and loneliness, yet follow. Follow because the Lord has promised and His promise is still true "I will never leave you …" (Heb. 13:5). By faith follow because there is something inside of you that continues to let you know you are not alone in the midst of your situation whatever it might be.

With that in-between place many times comes fear. You may feel like you don't feel fear but many people fear what they don't know. Everyone know where they have been but, they are unsure of where they are going, what to expect, what will it be like or even what will happen once they arrive at that place.

Although there should be comfort in knowing that Jesus is with you somehow you yet find yourself with just a little fear. Trusting in someone that you say you love, someone that you submit as well as commit your life to, should not be difficult but many people recognize they yet experience some fear. When you are willing to follow even if it is in fear you can yet be blessed because of your obedience in following the savior. It is not mere man that you follow but who it is that man follow, therefore by faith we follow. This one that we follow is Christ, the anointed one of God. Jesus made sure to let those that choose to follow him know what they could truly expect "Foxes have holes, and birds of the air have nests; but the Son of man hath not where to lay his head" (Luke 9:57). Your decision to follow Christ must be by faith because if you are not willing to look pass the things you are seeing with your natural eyes and not see Christ, but hear Christ calling to you to follow him then your faith level is not where it should be and need to be to follow him by faith. There is so much calling out to you in the spirit, beckoning you to follow Jesus to the other side. You must be willing to stop going by what you see don't worry about the winds just keep following Jesus by faith.

It is Jesus the Christ that can calm your storm. The ship of life may be rocking but by faith hear the call of Jesus saying follow me. Jesus said, "no man, having put his hand to the plough, and looking back, is fit for the kingdom of God" (Luke 9:62). Jesus sees the suitability in you to take you forward in your faith and your walk with him. Speak to your self and remind yourself that going back and looking back is not an option. It is your expected future that the master is asking you to following him to. He is not just pointing you in a direction to go, he is leading you. He said come let us cross to the other side. Jesus wants you to follow him, he at one point said, "…come take up the cross and follow me" (Mark 10:21). First he invited you to come, and then he asked you to follow him. All these things are faith acts because when he said come, faith and obedience will help you make a choice. Then he said follow me, again, faith and obedience is required as you make your choice. What will your choice be? Remember that you are in an in-between place and in that in-between place there are times you will have to bear your cross. Also keep in mind that Jesus has victory over the cross and because Jesus has victory you have victory also through him. When you put your hand to the plough please keep in mind that you don't take the plough backward but forward. You are encouraged to follow because the Lord will not start anything that he will not finish. According to scripture, it is necessary that you be confident in the fact that "he which hath begun a good work in you will perform (complete) it until the day of Jesus Christ" (Phil. 1:6). What must be realized is the fact that it takes faith to follow in a place and to a place that you can't see. Therefore, in your in-between place follow Jesus by faith to the place that he is taking you. You have come too far from where you were and you are too close to where He is taking you to stop now therefore I say to you, by faith follow. It is not necessarily about where you are but where you allow Jesus to take you. By faith just keep moving in the direction that Jesus is leading you. As long as Jesus is leading, and it is he that is with you don't be afraid to follow Him.

Your joy, your peace, God's love, and your assignment are all in your future. Jesus holds the plans of God that has been designed especially by him for your life and your future. Therefore by faith follow him through your in-between place, carry your cross and don't worry about the winds or the waves, Jesus is leading you to the other side. It is him that is able to keep you from falling while you are going through following him.

God's Mandate

There is one thing for certain about that place called in-between; going back is not an option. Every person that has found themselves right in the middle of this place must be able to make a conscious decision to press to move forward. Although sometimes it may feel like you are alone just remember the promise of the Father and of Jesus, I won't leave you, (Deut. 31:6; Heb.13:5). The determination to move forward must be in you.

Apostle Paul said it best "I press"(Phil. 3:14). Many of the blessings of God don't always come easy but, as long as you have the master right there with you, you can make it. There will be times that you may not be able to see him with your natural eye, he just might be in the rear of your spiritual ship, out of sight, allowing you the chance to lean on your faith but you must remember the author of Peace and the one that has the authority to do exceeding and abundantly above all you can ask or even think is there with you.

When God has an assignment for you, you can't allow what you see, or think you see, to dictate to you what the end will be. Remember to stick with your assignment, what has he told you to do. Again the Apostle Paul encourages the people of God to trust him. I Corinthians 10:13 gives those encouraging words, just what you need to use your faith and trust your master, "There hath no temptation taken you but such as is common to man: but God is faithful, who will not suffer you to be tempted above that you are able; but will with the temptation also make a way to escape, that ye may be able to bear it".

It does not matter how long you have had a relationship with the Father, the master, the savior, we yet have a problem sometimes with trusting him to fulfill his word to us. No, you don't won't to admit it but just the same it is true. God has purpose for each of his people and He loves us all and he wants to fulfill the plan that he has for our lives. Even now it might be a good thing to ask the Father to forgive you for not trusting him as you should, for the many times you questioned if things would work out. If we would really set back and give it some thought the problem for many of us is not God's fulfillment of his promise but our timing. We want things when we want it, how we want it, where we want it, and the way we think we should receive it. God forgive each of us for our selfish ways and the mistrust we have shown you, please forgive, we ask in Jesus' name.

Jeremiah 29:11 NLT

"For I know the plans I have for you, says the Lord. They are plans for good and not for disaster, to give you a future and a hope."

God has a plan for his people and has entrusted them with that plan. This plan is his mandate, a mandate that will give his people a future and a hope. He does not give anyone something that they can't handle with his help.

What God has planned is to bring those that will trust him to a place away from a destructive life style, through an in-between place, to the other side of it all. A place of love, joy, and peace in the Holy Ghost. A place where you can walk in the manifold blessings of the Lord just knowing that you are not alone in whatever you face in this life. You will be able to know that you have someone that love you more than you love yourself, someone that want only the best for you in this life and after.

The storm that you see on the outside is or may become a storm on the inside. Your storm is not so much natural as it is spiritual. Your in-between place, with its' winds and rain, is not the things you are seeing with your eyes but an inside shaking of the spirit. Your soul (mind, will, and emotions) is all over the place and there is a need for Jesus to speak peace to your soul. You can't fully please God until there is peace in your soul.

Everything that is going on to fulfill the master's plan for your life may not and many times will not be things that you see the victory in, because it is not a natural victory you seek, but learn victory in, because it is not a natural victory you seek, but learn in the midst of the storm to just stand still until the master's will is clear. Tell yourself that you will stay right where you are in the middle of your storm, determined that you won't move until you know the perfect will of God, his mandate, in your life and for your life.

It is important to recognize when God has a mandate on your life (and he does), he will make sure his mandate is accomplished. This accomplishment is being fulfilled through everything that happens in your life. It is not just one certain thing that may be done which fulfills his mandate but it is your life itself. Your life with its' ups and downs, its' successes and failures, they all come together and work together to fulfill the things that God has entrusted to you as steps to carry out that mandate on your life for that hope and future that is in his plan for you. God already has a mandate for your life. His mandate has been planned from your birth until your transition from earth to glory. But it is up to you to prayerfully walk out his plan through the process of your in-between place, step by step. Do you always know God's plan for you? No, not in the beginning but as you grow in him and submit yourself unto him, stay in his word, seek it out and pursue it, you will mature and this maturity will cause his plan to begin unfolding before you when you begin to know God's mandate also know that God is your light (Ps. 27:1), and also recognize that his word is able to light your path (Ps. 119:105), and it will if you will allow it. Make up your mind that you will move forward in the things of the Lord conquering the things that seem like they are impossible. Long for God's mandate in your life, long to know that every day you are walking the process that will cause this mandate to be what will take you through every storm, strengthening you and encouraging you.

Seek purpose in God's mandate for the change given to you, will it be the change that will fulfill your joy, is it what causes you to be empowered to stand firm in your faith and encourage the faith of others. God know every point in your life and at what point you will be ready for transition which will open you up for a transfer straight from the throne room of God. God will give you the transfer you will need to allow his mandate to be carried out in your life.

When you look at God's mandate you will hear God asking you to help someone else be blessed through your ability to carry out you mandate. If you are willing to carry out your assignment and you want to be blessed too, be willing to give of yourself. If you are willing to give to others God will give unto you. Listen to Jesus' assignment to Peter, "Simon, son of Jonah, lovest thou me more than these? Feed my lambs"(John 21:15). Jesus ask Peter the same question three times with the same instructions and each instruction was based on Peter's love for the Lord. In order to fulfill your mandate you must truly love the Lord because it will take more than, just want to, to fulfill God's mandate, it will take a true love for Jesus. When you really love the Lord with your whole heart you will be able to feed others in the will of God. Peter's ability to feed others was based on his love for Jesus. Our instructions from Jesus is "thou shalt love the Lord thy God with all thy heart, and with all thy soul, and with all thy mind" (Matt. 22:37). Not only do you have to love the Lord but we must love others (vs. 39) also, you can't you can't help others if you don't love them and Jesus knew this and it is why I believe he gave each of us the command to love our neighbor as ourselves.

It is our love for God that will help us to push pass obstacles that cross our path to do the will of God that he be glorified and we be blessed. It is in our sowing of our love and our time that God will look on us and allow that seed to bring forth a harvest. Don't you want a harvest for your labor? Then, labor for the harvest of the spiritual. Jesus says "Labor not for the meat which perisheth, but for that meat which endureth unto everlasting life, which the Son of man shall give unto you for him hath God the Father sealed" (John 6:27), with Jesus' instructions of the natural and the spiritual comes the encouragement of not asking for the natural. In I King 3:5-13 God rewarded Solomon because he desired the spiritual things of God. You too can have the great things of God both natural and spiritual when your concern is for the spiritual things of God. This is important because your mandate will rely on the spiritual things of God.

God is such a loving Father and Jesus a loving merciful savior that want the best for his people. Please understand that in the process of preparing you for his mandate, the Lord has to equip you through stretching you and allowing you to go through trials and tribulations all to help you to be better by trusting him and building your faith in his word. Faith that he will do what he says he will do and knowing that you can stand on every promise and it shall come to pass. Now seek him out so that you can know the true mandate of God for your life that you may be able to receive every blessing.

Overcoming Doubt

When you are in that in-between place there will be times when it feels like you are facing an impossibility, when the storms of life are causing the waves to rise high. But, remember that the calm will come when you are able to see and understand clearly the scripture that says, "I can do all things through Christ"(Phil. 4:13). This is a good time to remember that Jesus encouraged his followers concerning storms, in St. John 16:33 he tells them "These things I have spoken unto you, that in me ye might have peace. In the world ye shall have tribulation: but be of good cheer; I have overcome the world." Jesus was telling his followers they would have tribulations meaning storms but He (Jesus) has overcome the things of the world.

Therefore I say to you the calm begins to take place when you choose to believe, and have faith in, Jesus' promise. It is Jesus promise that will encourage you in speaking into your own self, that you can do all things because it is through Christ that makes all things possible. Jesus is right in the middle of the storm continuing to tell you, I will never leave you. He then speaks to your storm, Peace be still.

Much of the time the loss of hope causes the people of God to not see Christ right in the middle of their situations. We serve a God that is not flesh and blood that you have to work at getting him to come near to you, but a God that is spirit. This same God that is spirit is just as real as anything or anyone that you have ever known and his spirit is in you walking with you, living in you, waiting for you to recognize He is right there longing for you to live like he is there.

Live like he is there by talking to Him and listening to Him to hear what He by his spirit is saying to you. Then, walk in obedience to him and not be afraid. The people of God must stop seeing him as a God that is far away, but a God that is within. He is Christ in you, the hope of glory (Colossians 1:27). Began praying that Jesus will reveal himself to you that you may know him in a way that you have never known him before. When Jesus spoke to His disciples "let's cross to the other side"(Mark 4:35), He was right in the midst of them in the ship. Jesus was not on the other side waiting for them but with them. When the storm arose they went to Jesus in the ship and talked with him and this same Jesus is your "very present help"(Psalm 46:1), he is not somewhere waiting for you to invite him to come to your rescue for where ever you are he is there, now talk to him because he is listening.

Your in-between place is a place of transition, you have left from where you were but you haven't arrived at the place where you are headed, hold on as the storms arise and trust the master that he will ride through the storm and the winds of transition with you, your end results will be so much better.

Your in-between place is there to help you know, walk, live and carry out God's will and the plan He has for your life. The transition that Jesus is preparing you for is one that will equip you for a great transfer. The transition of Jesus, to take you to the other side, is one that comes with your determination to yield to all that he say do with expectation of a better way in your life. Also a better means of getting there is through persistence. If you are persistent to get all that Jesus has for you, you will get it. His plans for you are of peace and not of evil Jesus' desire is to bring you to an expected future. The ability to slow down, take a deep breath, and relax in your trust in the love of Christ will allow you to get through the storms and arrive at the other side. The other side of your fears, the other side of your pain and abuse. The emotional pain and the mental pain. Yes, and so much heartache that comes through the inability to trust more completely and just walk by faith.

You are finding yourself struggling for a more intimate relationship with Christ. Be reminded of the promises of God when you find yourself struggling. Exodus 6:7 says "And I will take you to me for a people, and I will be to you a God: and ye shall know that I am the Lord your God, which bringeth you out from under the burdens of the Egyptians." We are God's people and that is why He has planned and prepared a future for his people. The promise that awaits each of us on the other side of what we encounter while we struggle. Become personal with the Lord and allow him to align your life with his will. Consider the following as a means to allowing this alignment to begin and your relationship to become greater.

Lord I desire as I struggle in this place called in-between that you will be with me bringing change, new insight, and a craving for the more of you. Lord, that you will help me to see you better and that my love for you will grow stronger than it has ever been before. I'm hungry for you Lord, for the more of your refreshing and the more of your will in me. That I'm able to recognize you moving in me. That I understand more clearly what you are speaking to me and there be no doubt that you are leading me and directing me. Fill my hunger Lord, fill my thirst and please Lord, fill my longing to be close to you and that I know you are there, living in me, moving and directing me in you.

Don't allow the doubts that sometimes hunts me day by day to overcome me. I know that you are greater and doubt will become a weapon that I give the adversary to use against me if I don't release all this to you. I acknowledge this doubt in my life and I bring it to you that I may overcome it and be led by your word that tells me "finally my brethren be strong in the Lord and in the power of his might" (Eph. 6:11). I'm able to overcome the doubt that hunts me through the power that I find in you. Your power allows me to put on what I need and it helps me to allow you to help me take off of me every hindering cause that has planted itself upon me in the form of doubt. Today I'm overcoming doubt that I may walk in freedom in Jesus' name. I recognize that if I'm going to overcome the doubt that haunts me it is a process that I'm willing to go through. Today is the day that I have made up my mind that my overcoming process, will began. The "ing" on my overcome tells me it is a process, but Lord I'm willing and I'm determined. No longer do I choose to walk in the spirit of doubt. Doubt only causes me to miss some of what God has for me because when I allow doubt to have a place in my life then I'm choosing not to believe. I can't doubt and believe too. Therefore I choose to believe, believe everything that the word of God says to me. If God says something is mind then I will believe and confess that it belongs to me in Jesus' name. The word of God tells me if I can believe in my heart and not doubt, I can have whatsoever I ask (Matt. 21:21; Mk. 11:23). Therefore, not only have I decided to overcome doubt but also I choose to speak into my own life and believe, that I may have.

Know Thyself

While traveling through the North Carolina and Tennessee mountains so many things came to mind as I thought about this in-between place we encounter. In North Carolina the Blue Ridge Mountains were beautiful but I began to feel closed in as I went through them and there were the warning signs to watch out for deer and for the grade of steepness of the mountain. I mention those things because it caused me to think of the warnings given to each of us through the word of God, warnings to sustain us from the snares of the adversary. We are instructed to put on the whole armor of God that we may be able to withstand against the wiles
(schemes) of the devil. As I was going through the mountains there were many curves going up the mountains and while going up you could sometimes feel the car pulling harder to go up the steep mountains, not hills, but big mountains. Then there were the times when I was going down the mountains and the car would pick up speed wanting to go faster than the speed limits required. This is the way it can be sometime as the schemes of the devil is thrown at us as we go through our in-between place.

There are the times you strain just to get through a day of your in-between place. You can feel the tug on your mind and your emotions as you cry out to God just to get you through the next mountain. Thinking within yourself that it is just too hard and you feel so tired of the press with no deliverance in sight. These are some of your spiritual Blue Ridge Mountains. But then you realize that you still have the Great Smoky Mountains to encounter. In the great smoky' the curves are much steeper and the mountains are much deeper and so much higher. It seemed as I traveled through the Great Smoky Mountains I was being engulfed by the trees. The signs that warned of the possibility of falling and sliding rocks from the mountains were at every other curve. That is the way it is in our lives, it seems as though Satan is trying to throw something unexpected out at you as you go through your in-between place. Some things are beyond your control and you don't know when a test will come unexpected out of nowhere but you know who has control of it all, the master Jesus.

It is important to just stay in your lane of this spiritual trip into your in-between place. I have a saying that I often use which says, "I'm going to stay in my lane because if I don't I may run into some oncoming traffic and I don't know how fast that traffic may be going and it might cause an accident." It is enough to work hard at staying prayerful to trust Jesus to help you to stay in your lane making sure you don't cross no lines as you go through your mountains and around your curves of life. It is important to keep your trust in the Lord because you don't know what awaits you in that lane that is not for you to be in.

Trusting Jesus should be easy but it is not always because even though you have not been in this in-between place before, self always want to think that it knows what is best. I once heard or read the saying, trusting the Lord is a moment-by-moment choice. Therefore every one of us has to make it a practice of trusting the Lord in every part of our life and in every choice that is placed before us. When sailing through the storms of life, allow the spirit of the Lord to guide you through treacherous waters, as you move through the turbulent streams with him. You can't allow yourself to focus on what area of the in-between you may be in at that moment, whether it is a mountain, a curve, a stream, lane, or ship. Just focus on the fact that Jesus, the master of any condition or any element is with you and he has the power and the authority to speak not only to your situation but to any situation and it has to come subject to the master of all. Always remember that Jesus holds all power, in heaven and in earth, Hallelujah.

This is not just things that we say but they are the things that we believe with our whole heart as we trust the Lord to do what we need, and as we speak with the expectation that it shall be done. Jesus asked the blind men, "believest thou that I am able to do this? Then he said according to your faith be it unto you" (Matt. 9:28-29). Now just think about it, when you truly believe that Jesus has the power and the authority to do what you are asking of him then you expect it to be done. Expectation that is based on your faith is the reason why you should find trusting Jesus easy. Now examine yourself, do you believe what you say that you believe? The in-between place can seem long and many times it is long, but it should not keep you from trusting the one that love you enough to die for you, in spite of yourself. He (Jesus) said "I love you with an everlasting love…" this should give you reason enough to trust him, especially when you know that he can't lie.

Every day I tell the Lord "Lord I trust you", it is not based on how things are going on that day or in my life, it is based on all that he has already done for me. I recognize the more I tell Jesus that I trust him the more it becomes a part of me in every situation. I know above all else, I trust the Lord. I can rest in knowing that I trust God. Be it God, Jesus, Holy Ghost, Master, Savior, or Lord, one thing I know is I trust Him. I don't have to second-guess it I know that I trust Him, what about you, can you say with assurance that you trust Him? When you can have that kind of assurance you can rest in knowing that better days are ahead of you. No matter what each day present you will be able to face the day knowing that whatever you are faced with it is going to work for your good and lead you to the plan that he has for your life.

Every mountain and every valley has been placed in your path to help you become who you have been ordained before your birth, to be. Every lonely night and all the times you have been falsely accused the master see and he care when it seems as though no one care. For every tear that has fallen from your eyes and no one but the savior saw them, He care and He will remember your days and your nights that you have sought, to know thy own self, while seeking to trust him through it all. Remember, your savior loves you with a never-ending love and for you he died so don't worry about a little pain now because a better day is coming. The tears, the pain and heartache that you may experience now is gently pushing you through your in-between place to the other side, the place that Jesus, the master, Lord and savior has asked you to go. It is up to you to make the choice to trust him and go or stay right where you are.

When anyone becomes grateful enough for all that has truly been done for them the choice is an easy one to make but there is yet and will remain to be an in-between place that every person will have to go through. The difference will be when you choose to trust Jesus you will not go through your in-between place alone for Jesus will be right there with you lovingly going through the in-between place with you. It is knowing that Jesus knows every pain and every heartache you experience. There is nothing that he does not know about you and still he cares so lovingly for you. Now make your choice, choose to accept the invitation of Jesus to come and cross to the other side with him.

It is clear that the in-between place must be traveled because it is the path to the other side. If you don't know what it is that will help you trust Jesus I will tell you it is knowing and keeping before you what Jesus has done just for you, because He loves you. Knowing and loving Jesus will help you to know thyself. Yes, knowing Jesus will help you to know thyself but it is important to be true to thyself. Being true is to not pretend you are something that you know you are truly not. It is when you are able to face the likes and the dislikes about your own self and acknowledge this is who I really am, I don't like this or that about myself but it is who I truly am. Next in line is to make a choice about what you are willing to do that you don't remain the same, if you don't like what you see.

The scripture says, "…man looketh on the outward appearance, but the Lord looketh on the heart"(I Samuel 16:7). Therefore, in examining your own self you must truly seek God to show you your heart and be willing to work toward life and your life with Christ based on what is in your heart. It is not always easy to truly take a look at yourself, seeking God to show you what it is that he see as he look at your heart.

When you really want to know thyself you can't make

excuses for what you see that is not God pleasing, or for the things that are lacking in areas of your life. But the true key of even trying to know thyself is to be able to see the short comings and long to be that person that says Lord help me, I need your help to change the things that I can with a willing heart and be willing to release me to you Lord that you do what you want to do with me. I yield my will to you, totally to you Lord.

There are so many people that proclaim to be a child of the most high God but that same child wants to stay in that comfort zone that they have made for themselves. If and when you truly want to get through your in-between place and arrive at the other side, that place the master has called you to, you must be willing to search yourself, acknowledge who you truly are, that you may get to know thyself with God's help, then be willing to move forward. Some of the places you will encounter may be uncomfortable, you won't be able to stay in your comfort zone and allow your flesh to control the way that you live life.

To know thyself, you have to know your weak areas as well as your strong areas. You need to know if you are able to give thanks when things are not going the way you expect them to go. Don't find yourself in fear and doubt when you encounter life's raging storms, which would be weak areas in your spiritual walk. Much of the weak areas in one's life is created by fear. In St. Mark 4, the disciples thought they were about to die in the storm (v.38) but Jesus knew the authority that he had, not just over the storm, but also over the entire sea. After calming the storm Jesus asked his disciples a question that would make them search themselves, "why are ye so fearful? How is it that ye have no faith?" (v. 40).

If someone would have ask the disciples about their faith they may have said they had faith but it is important to know thyself, not just think you do but have an assurance of who you truly are. Although Jesus was in the boat with the disciples when the storm came they were fearful. When life causes you to fear in the things you should be trusting in your savior for, you need to take inventory of where your faith is. Things come many times to show us who we are and where we are in our relationship with our savior. It is in these times that every person should consider where their faith is in the Lord, again it is important to truly know thyself, not just think that you do.

You may be wondering if you will ever truly know thyself but it is the storms of life that come, which will help you continue to take inventory of your own self. In every storm that life bring our way it gives each of us another opportunity to trust in Jesus and it will also give Jesus the opportunity as we trust in him to reveal his presence as well as his compassion to each of us. Just as Jesus had control over the storm of the sea he also has control over every storm that we may encounter in our lives. If you are not careful your fear will cause you to doubt what Jesus can and will do in your life. But, if you don't know thyself you will not recognize when fear is operating in your life.

Jesus will help you to know thyself through your own life situations. Just as the two blind men that wanted to receive their sight when they approached Jesus he help them to take a look at their own faith as he questioned them "Believe ye that I am able to do this? According to your faith be it unto you"(Matt. 9:28-29). This is just one reason why it is important to know thyself, because many times your blessing or your deliverance is based on you knowing yourself. You need to know if your faith is where you think it is because your deliverance may just depend on it.

The children of God has such assurances in their walk with Christ if they will only pay attention to the promises of God. One assurance that has been given to the followers of the Lord is "Fear thou not; for I am with thee: be not dismayed; for I am thy God: I will strengthen thee; yea, I will help thee; yea, I will uphold thee with the right hand of my righteousness"(Isa. 41:10). It is important to keep reminding one's self of whom we serve. As I refer to Jesus it is as savior but I also think that it is important for people to make him their Lord. When you decide to say I want to truly know myself, who I am and what

I truly believe without doubt, then ask yourself if you have made Jesus your Lord. Jesus paid the ultimate price to be your savior but only you can allow him to be your Lord. When you allow Jesus to be Lord of your life it will not be a problem to trust him and be willingly obedient to him. The assurance is there for you and you don't have to fear because you have a father and a savior that is there for you that want what is best for you. You can't find a greater love than has been shown to you through God the Father and Jesus His son. "For God so loved the world, that he gave his only begotten son…"(John 3:16). Jesus has a declaration which says "my Father, which gave them me, is greater than all…I and my Father are one…and I lay down my life"(John 10:15, 29-30). Great sacrifice has been made for every person in the world it is up to you to decide how you will respond to the gift that has been given to you.

The point that I would like for you to have an understanding of is in beginning to know thyself, you must make the decision if Jesus is your Savior only or if you have made the choice of allowing him to be your Lord and walk in true obedience to your Lord, as I stated before. Don't allow the fear of not knowing to hinder the decisions that only you can make for yourself. Fear is a spirit but if you allow it to entertain you it will become a weapon that the enemy will use against you to control you.

Know thyself whether you have been delivered from the things that has kept you from moving forward with Christ or if you, at this point, is willing and ready to repent to the Lord and make this your day of walking wholeheartedly with Christ. Know thyself and because you do, let this be a new day in your life and your relationship with Christ that gives you the peace that surpasses what you within yourself can't understand. When you allow Christ to be your lord you will be real and you will ask him to help you in your weak areas and this is acknowledging that you have weak areas in your life. This is acknowledging before the Lord that you are willing to be transparent and walk in humility before him. When you seek to know thyself, seek to know what kind of ground you are, what is your spiritual soil like? Are you the ground that is stony? When the word of the Lord is given are you one that is glad for the word and seem happy but when trouble or trails come you are easily offended and the word is of no affect in you. You look around and find yourself sinking because you don't really know thyself. Maybe you are the ground that is producing thorns and the things of life takes priority over the word of God in you. You think that you are able to stand in your in-between place but your things are choking out the word of God that you thought was planted deep enough in you to keep you. But, you realized that you didn't know thyself.

Maybe you truly are good ground and you now recognize it is not that you have been so good but it is because as you were taking inventory of yourself you realized that you need Christ every day in everything. Reflecting back on the word of God in you, you began to remember that you have a savior that love you and is there for you, one that has never lied to you and He can't lie. A savior that is there to keep you from falling. You are good ground because you checked to know thyself and found that although you have many faults, you have a savior that is able to present you faultless. This is because of what he has done for you, the price he has paid for you through his shed blood. Therefore you accepted this Jesus as savior, and you have allowed him to be Lord. For these reasons you stand as good ground.

When you strive to know thyself you realize that the only way you are able to get through this in-between place and truly know thyself is because Jesus the Christ is the difference needed in your life. It is Jesus that makes your soil good because it has been enriched by the blood of Jesus and whatever is planted in that spiritually blood rich soil will take root and grow because of that blood. In this sense you will be able to acknowledge; this is who I truly am because of the blood. I am good ground. When you seek to know thyself it is not who you want others to think you are but allow them to see the real you, the one with some depth, one that is able to stand the storms that will come through time and make it to the other side. Now can you say that you truly know thyself or have you taken the time to check? It is important to know thyself and you will never be deceived by the adversary. Know who you are and whose you are. To know thyself is to move forward in the things of God.

Desire

Desire has a lot to do with you walking out the process that has been designed to take you to that place God has planned for your life. You must desire to follow through to that place the Lord has for you. You can't really see the place that you are in nor can you see the place that has been ordained just for you that is awaiting you in your future. Desire will help you as you walk out this process to get there. Depending on how strong your desires may be they can get you to where you need to be, the other side. Just knowing that it is the will of Jesus to take you to the other side, and this alone should give you a strong desire to get there. If Jesus has said it, your desire to get there should be great. Nothing is easy nor does it come easy but you should long to get to the place that Jesus wants to take you. He said come let us go to the other side and that alone says he is with you or you are with him, otherwise, Jesus would have said go to the other side. It also will let you know that it is he that is leading and you are following.

There was a song once that said, I have decided to follow Jesus, no turning back, no turning back. Wherever Jesus leads be willing to follow. How you follow will also depend on your desire. When you have a desire, you truly crave to have or do something therefore, you will willingly put forth more effort toward whatever it is that you desire.

When there is a desire to do the will of God or first of all to know God's will for your life you begin to work tirelessly toward doing the things that he just might be leading you to do. Because you are not sure you continue to pray about what his will for your life maybe. Working hard at just this one thing can cause you to become exhausted in your mind and confused. One thing that may help when you can't seem to get the clarity you need concerning God's will for your life, you should learn how to relax, which may not be easy, and not work at what you think is being faithful and obedient. This does not mean not to do anything but allow your mind to not become so stressed with knowing the answer quickly.

As you, through prayer and meditation, relax in the Lord his will for you will become clearer and you will be able to move forward in the things of God. Many times the desires of one's heart can cause one to try so hard to do the will of the Lord that things become blocked and you began to just go in circles not truly accomplishing anything.

Take time to stop and recognize that the adversary wants to wear you out. Although you mean well and you are trying to walk in obedience and do the right thing the adversary can cause you to become mentally exhausted and spiritually discouraged. These are a few things that can cause you to become discouraged and get off track. The word of God has some encouraging words for the people of God that may be a little rocky in trying to fulfill the desire they may have. In Galatians 6:9 it says "And let us not be weary in well doing: for in due season we shall reap, if we faint not." You must stop and take the time to recognize that God is a God that know all things and he know that you truly love him and desire to please him therefore don't lose heart you will not lose your reward.

Stop, and take the time to give some thought about what you really long to do and feel really lead to do for the Lord, that gives him glory. As you seek out your desire think how the scripture speaks of desire "one thing have I desired of the Lord, that will I seek after; that I may dwell in the house of the Lord all the days of my life, to behold the beauty of the Lord, and to inquire in his temple"(Ps. 27:4). This scripture reminds us that the things we desire we will seek after them and the things you continuously seek after you will receive. Mark 11:24 says "Therefore I say unto you, what things soever ye desire, when ye pray, believe that ye receive them, and ye shall have them."

As you are reminded of his word remember to pray for your heart's desire and began to walk in expectation of your heart's desire. Yes, and my soul desire is to love the Lord more and more every day. My desire is to be so close to Jesus that my relationship with him is like white in rice, any way you break the grain of rice you see white. With white rice you can't separate the white and the rice. I don't want anything to be able to come between me and Jesus. I desire that there be nothing that will be able to make me doubt my savior.

I pray that you have begun to rethink your desires and recheck to see if in your desires the Lord is first. Do you desire Jesus to be first in your life or is he just thrown in there somewhere? Learn to develop a hunger for the Lord. Let your desire be so great that you hunger day by day for the more of him and your relationship with Jesus will become greater. If you don't have a relationship with Jesus let your desire be that you develop a relationship with him.

You must be willing to desire something from the Lord. He desires something from you. Let your desire be that your life will be changed and that you never be the same again, that you walk in his love day by day. Allow yourself to desire for others also, that they too will desire the greater in the Lord. Desire that homes and relationships will be mended, that families be delivered and Christ be the head as his spirit rule in the hearts and minds of mothers and fathers, sons and daughters. Allow your desire alone to be able to see the glory of God being manifested, even greater than it now is. That it be manifested in and through his people and that the world may be able to clearly see it too. That through you God's glory become that light to the world, shinning unto everlasting life.

There are many desires that this society may and do have, but just allow room for God to be included in those things that you desire. I don't want anyone to think that I feel like you should only desire God and Him only. We desire other things such as cars, houses, clothes, certain types of foods, etc. but just don't forget about God. Also be mindful to teach the children and the youth how to desire the things of God. Tell them how the things of God, when it is their greatest desire, will keep them in the things they will encounter as youth in the Lord and it will help them to be a light to draw other youth to Christ.

There is not a list of desires that I can give to say this is what your desires should be but I do know that as you seek him and live for him your desires will come and they will multiply. Then you will get to a place where you will begin to say, one thing have I desired of the Lord. Then it will be another and another, your desires will grow as you grow and only you and God will know what those desires will be. Remember the Lord wants you to desire things of him. Never be afraid to acknowledge your desires to your savior and as you mature in him the desires will change. As you are maturing in these things also learn how to be patient because everything doesn't come over night but it does not mean that it will not come. Jesus gave reason for everyone to exercise patience as he said,

"In your patience possess ye your souls"(Luke 21:19). Keep in mind that you don't have to doubt God nor do you need to rush God. He know when you need, those things that you desire. "For he satisfieth the longing soul, and filleth the hungry soul with goodness"(Psalm 107:9). The Lord will fulfill these desires and for this cause the Psalmist also says "Oh that men would praise the Lord for his goodness, and his wonderful works to the children of men"(v. 8). Again for what he does for us, He alone is worthy to be praised.

My Battle of an In-Between Place

Your in-between can be in many different places and many different ways. I have experience various in-between places in my life, places that caused me to be shaken to the very core of my soul.

Living and experiencing a spiritual war within my own mind, of my labor in the Lord, if it has been pleasing to him or have I continuously fell short of his will and his word. To preach in the anointing and being able to see souls blessed of the Lord. To behold God move by his power and show himself mighty and I've cried out in prayer for those that came to me seeking prayer and answers to their unanswered questions. Yet, I often wondered if in my service to the Lord, had I did enough to please God.

God is not a God that we have to labor in fear, afraid to misstep and be destroyed. But God is our Lord, and we should always be mindful that at the name of Jesus we should give reverence to the most high. I set and wonder how many times have I preached or prayed and just assumed that God would answer and his power would be in display to the people and there would be no reason for any to doubt. Now I search myself and I wonder did I pray through humble submission or just assumed if I asked he would do it. I don't think that either is bad but humbleness before the Most High God is important and it is also important to pray in the will of God. Understand that it is a difference between assuming a thing or, just asking in faith that it is the will of your savior to grant the request that you seek of him.

Seeking the will of God is important in what decision you make. I'm grateful that the Lord granted the request that I placed before him but in hindsight I wondered if I was truly pleasing in his sight. I remember on one occasion a young lady dropped to the floor in one of the services and died. Without any thought I sat down in the floor and lifted up her upper body in my arms and held her and began to rebuke death in the name of Jesus, seeking God to bring this woman back to life. Somewhere within me I believed God to bring her back to life. Stand in the gap, I truly believed God was going to give this young lady her life back, and I know that I had faith but this is also a time that I assumed that God in Jesus' name was going to do just what I had asked of him, no doubt. Standing boldly to declare the things of God and the things that I believed he was imparting unto me without fear. Although the spirit of the Lord was moving through me, in hindsight there were things that also held my attention and now I can see that I allowed people and things to hold some of my attention that truly belonged to God. God yet moved and showed himself mighty to the people. People were being healed, many delivered and miracles were taking place. God gave revelation knowledge in advance of two years and allowed the parishioners of the church to see it come to pass. I held the belief that if God has said it, let's just do it, no excuse. Because this is the way that I strived to please God I believed that it could be done by others also. It was to say, if you love God you will do what his word says. Seek out what he wants in your life and pray, fast, and seek him for direction to accomplish his will. It was like having spiritual tunnel vision but now I truly see it was a battle for me in an in-between place. It is not easy to try and reveal the place God has moved me from, although many were blessed in many areas of their lives as well as receiving great knowledge. Now there came a time that I wanted out, after open-heart surgery and then five years after that, a massive heart attack, I just wanted out. But, you must know that God revealed to me that it was not and is not his will to release me from the assignment that he has given to me. I don't know if you have experienced anything like this in your walk with Christ or not but I want to assure you that God is faithful and He has a perfect plan for your life. Although you may experience that same feeling that I experienced I just wanted out of the place I was in, the city, it was not God's will. I moved away for ten months but God sent me back and it was right after my return that I had the massive heart attack. I just felt it was not for me but I didn't consider God, I was looking at my circumstances. You must know that God is greater than your circumstances. It is not because we say it but it is because it is true, God Is greater than any of our circumstances.

My in-between place caused me to feel distant from God and I could not seem to be able to hear God for the answers I needed to my unanswered questions. I don't doubt that God was and is speaking; I was having a problem hearing him the way that I was used to hearing him. Oh, the pain that can be found in an in-between place. In-between places can be different for many but when you long for God in an intimate way and he seem far from you and you love him with all your heart, it can be so painful but don't give up. Just continue to remember that Jesus love you more than you could ever imagine and he has promised to never leave you nor forsake you (Hebrews 13:5). Hold to what he has promised and remember that he can't lie (Titus 1:2). It is when you feel the farthest from the Lord that you need to remember his word and continue to remind yourself of what he has promised in his word.

It is not always easy to share the hurts and the battles of an in-between place but when you know that God has forgiven and God has delivered, you too will be able to share that some other soul can be blessed and delivered. You can only be delivered when you are ready to let go of that shortcoming and be open. God told me that I would live this book and I have struggled in many ways since I began to write but I have not given up. I know that God has a plan for my life and I'm determined to fulfill his plan, for in it are the blessings of God. I seek the overflow of God in my life.

Walking along one day praying and crying out to God just to hear his voice and to know his will for me he let me know that when I wanted out and I stop doing the work that he had given me to do, it was not his will for me to stop, yet he allowed it. Through tears I repented and made up my mind at that moment that anything God wanted me to do from that moment forward, that I would do. From the time of my repentance I have recognized that I have been in an in-between place and I'm yet striving and praying to get to the other side but this time I won't give up, I will remain faithful until he decide to assign to me what he has just for me. Maybe there is someone that can identify with what I'm experiencing in my in-between place. Maybe you too are in a similar in-between place and you are unsure what to do. Let me say, remain faithful don't give up, the storm that you feel like you are now in will not last always. Jesus, your savior, is right there riding through your storm with you. He will not allow you to sink but you must truly be willing to turn loose the weight that is holding you back, you know what it is, it's the thing you have been afraid to share because of people but

God is saying turn it loose, I will catch you. He is the one that is able to keep you from falling and present you faultless, not the people that you are so concerned about. See, when you allow him to deliver, you will be able to talk about it in the right place at the right time.

There are times that you may wonder why you can't hear God. Don't give up keep listening, the voice will come, in the way and the time that he chooses. Because you may not be hearing his voice in the way you desire, do as the Lord told me, "keep working and you will work your way into what I want you to do". This let me know that He is speaking. Stay faithful, keep working, He is going to bring you and me out with clarity of his will for our lives.

I believe that as the Lord bring each of us out of this in-between place, we will be so grateful that there will not be, hopefully, a problem with wanting to give up. He has been too good and has remained faithful to each of us and all we need is to be faithful to him. This in-between place is strengthening and equipping us for what he has for those that will obey. Scripture says "And we know that all things work together for good to them that love God, to them who are the called according to his purpose" (Romans 8:28) All that we go through and every place we are in, in some way it is working and strengthening us for our good.

Always keep in mind that it is not of ourselves but it is of

Christ that we can do this or that. Philippians says, "I can do all things through Christ which strengtheneth me" (4:13). Anything that we have been allowed to do is because of Christ and through Christ. Don't allow yourself to assume, as I did, that things are just going to happen when you ask but have faith that according to his will it shall be done and according to your faith. Never think that in-between places are easy but do remember that in-between places were not designed to stay in, they are designed to go through and they will lead you from one place to another.

When you find yourself in an in-between place it is because you have stepped from the shores of one place, headed to another but if you are in an in-between place it means that you have not yet arrived at your destination. But, don't drown or be carried away by the currents of an in-between place. It is important that you don't allow what you may see, hear or even what you may feel in your in-between place to distract you from trusting Jesus to bring you through to the other side. This has been just a small portion of an in-between place of mine. We do not always get delivered from our storm with a peace be still but sometimes God will take us through our storm with his promise of, I won't leave you nor forsake you. He will be right with you us as he hold our hand and safely guide us through. Either way God decide to deal with your storm just remember that he has a plan for your life and he will always do what he decide is best for that moment in your life.

Although each of us have our battles God will always determine the strategy that he wants to use for your present battle, your battle of an in-between place. If you are able to believe that he is working things out for your good, no matter what the outcome may seem like, it will always work for your good. You may not always get what you think you should have but just make sure that God always get the glory that he deserve.

I'm sure that I'm not the only one with a battle or several battles of an in-between place but it is your willingness to recognize your battles and a willingness to share some seeds of your battles and you will be able to recognize that you were never alone when the storms in your life were raging high and you never will be. You must stop at the onset of a battle and remember that Jesus is the peace in the middle of your storm; he is your bridge over your troubled waters, and the wheel in the middle of your wheel. The important thing that must be remembered at all times is although Jesus is Alpha and Omega, the beginning and the ending in your life you must also recognize that he is also right in the middle of your in-between place.

Jesus was there when you stepped away from the banks of commission headed to the banks of fulfillment, but while you are yet riding your Holy Ghost ship through the waters of assignment Jesus is still right there. Yes, in the waters of assignment the winds of gossip will blow and the clouds of whispering will form and the rain of discouragement will certainly fall, causing the chill of being unsure of your assignment, known as doubt, in your life.

If you could only imagine a God that love you so much that he would accept the life of His Son as payment for the price of your sin. If you could only imagine that one-day you will be able to behold the face of the one that died just for you and will always love you with an everlasting love in spite of yourself. Someone that does not see the outside of you but only looks at your heart. Now imagine this kind of friend, savior, and Lord, right in the middle of your battle and storm called in-between riding with you holding you up and holding you close. He loves you and he will keep you safe, if you will let him assuring that you will arrive at the bank of fulfillment giving God praise and glory for loving you so much, and bringing you safely in from the storm of your in-between place. He want you to trust him because he is able to do exceeding and abundantly above all that you could ever ask or think of him all because he loves you. Therefore I say unto you go ahead, face the battle of your in-between place as I face mine and know in your hearts that you don't fight this or any battle alone. You only find yourself in an in-between place because you have chosen to move forward in the things of the Lord. If you stand still you won't find yourself in between two given places of the Lord. Go ahead take the step and as you take the step he will step with you.

You see, it is in him that you and I live, move, and have our being. Therefore, I will lift up my head as I lift up my hands and my heart to my savior in this place that I now travel, called in-between, seeking with all that is within me to fulfill every assignment that has been placed in your hands. My precious sisters and brothers and fellow laborers in the gospel, there is no in-between place that you and I can encounter that Jesus is not there bringing us through.

It is the battle of my in-between place that help to teach me to forgive and that same battle has taught me to love in spite of as well as to humble myself. Many times your battle is not all bad but just maybe when you can stop and take a good look at the work your heavenly father is doing in you while you are in your in-between place you may decide that the battle of your in-between place can be seen as all good. All good because the father of your very soul is using your battle to work within you the will to take authority and press in to your storm and learn the lesson that the master want you to learn, that you will not become stuck in this place but you will be strengthen to come out on the other side of it all rejoicing in the Holy Ghost because you recognize that very battle was designed with your name on it. The father and master of your soul knew that you would not give up but would endure to the end that you could recognize that the Lord is good and your blessing and reward is on the other side of the battle of your in-between place.

God want you to trust Him. Yes, we say that we trust him but do you really trust Him? You must be able to recognize that the God you serve "is able to do exceeding abundantly above all that we ask or think, according to the power that worketh in us" (Eph. 3:20). You and I serve a God that has the whole world in His hands and there is nothing too hard for God. Battles will come and there will be in-between places that will arise in our time here on earth but God is well able to supply all our need. The battle of my in-between place was only a season and seasons come and seasons go but there will be a new day that will come bringing brand new mercies.

I have learned not to get stuck on the battle at hand but to keep in mind that the Lord's mercies are new every morning (Lam. 3:23). It's knowing that God is merciful that helps me to keep an attitude of total trust in the Lord. It has become a part of my inner being to trust God. Whatever arise I trust the Lord to do whatever I need to keep me in the place that I'm in and sweetly and swiftly move me to the next level.

In the word of God you can always find what you need for that season in your life. Jude says "Now unto him that is able to keep you from falling…" (V.24), therefore it is in your power to remind yourself as I do that, Jesus and the Holy Ghost is my keeper and I choose not to stumble. I choose to go through my battles with the assurance that I have a savior that is right there with me in whatever I'm going through. Jesus does not just go through my battle with me but he also understands the battle that I'm in, my hurts and the pain that comes as I endure sometimes. In my ups and downs, although I know he is with me, I have allowed myself at times to feel the loneliness that comes in that in-between place and that is why it is important to work toward staying focused. Broken focus can and will get you into trouble with self.

The mind is a large part and an important part of any battle. It is not so much the fear that comes with the battle because the spirit of fear will show up and it is important to be honest about what you are dealing with in your battlefield. If you are able to acknowledge that God has given you a word for your battle, "For God hath not given us the spirit fear; but of power, and of love, and of a sound mind" (II Timothy 1:7). When you or I take the step to acknowledge, this is not a spirit from the Lord. It will be at this point that you will know how to work to stop this spirit from going any further in this battle that you're in.

You begin by stirring up your gifts so that you may operate in the power that you have in the Holy Ghost (the spirit of the Lord), you do this in the spirit of love, although you're in a battle, you must operate in the love of God, because God is love. Then, you call to remembrance that God has given you a sound mind and you can't allow your battle to cause you to be shaken in the corners of your mind. God is there to keep each of us in perfect peace, he is well able but he want you to allow him to do it. All these things are attached to how you think, the mind.

If you are going to win the battle you must be able to think clearly. We can't rely on our own understanding, but we must trust the Lord to direct the paths that we take in our battles. Although I knew many times what I needed to do, there was that small part of me that just wanted to do what I wanted to do, such as putting those that were persecuting me, in their place. I know that you too have had the experience of praying and the more that you prayed the Lord would speak into your spirit as he did with me and say "trust me, I got this". If you have not experienced this, let me say, I have.

Once I was in Dallas, Texas and I open my mouth to make a comment and I didn't think that I was about to say anything wrong but, the Holy Ghost spoke into my spirit so profound and said "shut up", it shook me to the core. Believe me it is very important to be sensitive to the spirit of the Lord and know when He is speaking.

Jesus does not want any of us to become stuck in an in-between place. He came to set the captive free but do you want to be free, is the question you should ask yourself. Again, be honest with yourself, because God is looking at your heart. You will find it difficult to please self and God too. When you find yourself in a war, that battle that has come up in your soul realm, you might better count up the cost of trying to fight a battle that you have not forsaken all to Christ for. Don't expect to win but with Christ you can do all things because He has already won the battle a long time ago, at Calvary. Oh, I've had many battles in in-between places but I have learned to keep Jesus as my center and it keeps me from becoming stuck in the fight. It is in Him (Jesus), I live, move, and have my being.

Take the Time to Pray

When your storm becomes overwhelming don't panic, pray. If you take the time to acknowledge Him (Jesus), he will tell you what to do (Proverbs 3:6).

Instructions has been given to those who seek deliverance in their battle with storms. I Thessalonians 5:17 says "Pray without ceasing" with this instruction you must decide if you will walk in obedience to the instructions. It is in the middle of your obedience that your faith is tired the most but you must decide if you will continue moving forward through prayer exercising your faith in expectation.

To pray without ceasing is to keep an attitude of prayer. Every prayer is not on your knees crying out audibly, but within your spirit seek God to speak to your storm. God will do what you expect Him to do and what you will trust him to do. Seek to know more about the one you are praying to. The cry of the psalmist said "Hear my cry, O God; attend unto my prayer. From the end of the earth will I cry unto thee, when my heart is overwhelmed, Lead me to the rock that is higher than I; for thou has been a shelter for me, and a strong tower from the enemy" (Psalm 61:1-3).

Your heart need to be open to the God that you pray to and have an expectation as you go through the day that he is going to do something new for you and in you because you are expecting him to. It is in the middle of your believing that you should be watching for God to move. Your faith is challenged when the winds are high right in the midst of your in-between place. The winds and the waves may be high but Jesus is the controller of the winds and the waves. It was Jesus that spoke to a raging sea and said, "Peace be still" (Mark 4:39), and it obeyed Him. If three words from Jesus was able to calm the winds and waves then what would make you think he can't calm the raging sea that is trying to overtake you. If he did it then, he can and he will do it now because he is the same now as he was then (Hebrews 13:8). When you are in your in-between place ask yourself, where do I go from here? It is questions such as this that will cause you to go to God in prayer. While seeking God in prayer take the time to search yourself with questions that you need the Lord to help you answer, questions like, do I stay in this place that I'm in and drown or do I continue moving forward to my destiny. It is when you take the time to pray that you will also take the time to consider where you are and where you were going (Haggai 1:5 & 7), as well as where is it that you want to go.

Jesus said to count up the cost when you prepare to do something (Luke 14:28 & 31), but God has also informed you that he has a plan for your life, to bring you to an expected end (Jeremiah 29:11). It is up to you to make your decisions;

the Lord does not force anyone to do anything against their will. He speaks and allow you to decide what you want to do. Be reminded when making your decisions, you are dealing with a father that loves his children and any loving father wants what is best for his children.

You might say you want to follow but are you willing to follow. There are things that come when you are truly willing to follow the savior. There is a song that I use to sing which says "I have decided to follow Jesus, no turning back, no turning back", you might be saying at this moment, I have decided to follow Jesus too, but can you pay the price to follow, because He has paid the price to lead.

It takes obedience to follow but it took Jesus dying to lead. This is not about can you obey, it's about will you obey? No matter which decision you make He will yet love you. When you don't do what your friends want you to do many times or shall we say most of the time they will turn their backs on you but, when you decide to do the opposite of what Jesus is asking of you, you will find that he is right there, yet loving you and making intercession to our Heavenly Father just for you. Now that is not only a friend, that's love.

Now ask yourself again the same question, where do I go from here. Say to yourself again, I'm in my in-between place, but do I chose to follow or stay right where I am and drown or do I continue moving forward in you, Lord. I'm praying for your help. Be like the lepers and say "why sit we here until we die?" remember, there is nothing too hard for God, just take the time to pray and allow him to move. The solution for the discouragement and depressed state that many find themselves in as they travel through this place called in-between, is to look back on the many miracles God has provided for his people in their past. Thinking of His blessings will cause the raging sea of disappointment and the strong winds that are blowing at that moment to cease because the miracles of your past will stir the faith that you have for your future.

Remember Hebrews 10:32 & 35 and cast not away…your confidence. God want you to remember, therefore remember my brother and my sister and be blessed. Trust God to speak to your situation as you take the time to talk to him in prayer, and remember, there will be peace. Don't allow the situation to capture your attention for there will be storms but remember the words of the master. Your help is not on the way; it's in your midst, right there with you. You have no need to fear, just give Him praise and that praise will get his attention. Just think for a moment, you want deliverance, He wants praise.

To get to the other side, that place Jesus has commanded that you go, when he said "let us cross to the other side" (Luke 4:35), you must recognize that you have to leave your place called here, headed to a place called there. This is the journey you must see yourself on and after you have left the banks of here and before you get to your destination of there, you are in a place called in-between.

Don't get lost in this journey that you are on, it is important to stay focused on Jesus, through prayer, or the winds and the waves of life that are sent by the enemy to toss you will cause you to fear. At the point that you start to fear you will get off course, if you don't take the time to pray, allowing doubt to come in driving you father away from the place that Jesus want to take you.

Jesus is the only one that can get you safely to the other side. Continue to remember God's word, "I know the thoughts that I think toward you or the plans he has for you, they are of peace, God has said and not of evil. He has assured you that he wants to give you an expected future (Jeremiah 29:11), one that he already planned out for your life. Therefore, it is very important to stay focused on Jesus, on his word, and on his promise. If you loose focus you won't know where to go or how to get there. This is not based on you trying to figure this journey out; it's about trusting the Lord to stay true to his word (Proverbs 3:5-6).

When you are trusting the Lord and his word you must be willing at all times to pray. The palmist, David, took the time to pray what seems like a prayer in a time of true need. David says "Hear My cry, O God; attend unto my prayer. From the end of the earth will I cry unto thee, when my heart is overwhelmed, Lead me to the rock that is higher than I. For thou hast been a shelter for me, and a strong tower from the enemy" (Psalm 61: 1-3). You must know who you can turn to when you need them the most to sustain you in the middle of the storm. When you feel desperate and you are willing to take the time to approach God in prayer you truly need a shelter but you also need a strong tower. That tower is Jesus, the savior of the world, he will never fail thee.

The scripture in Matthew says, "watch and pray, that ye enter not into temptation…"(26:41). It is important for every person to be watchful. Be aware of your surroundings that you don't become caught in the web of the enemy. When you are going through certain situations in life and you don't take the time to seek the will of your heavenly father for your life, you will enter an area that will open you up to a spirit of bitterness and even anger. These kinds of spirits don't want you to see yourself in error but putting time into seeking God in prayer will help you come back to the place that will help you to say "Search me, O God, and know my heart."(Psalm 139:23). Don't ever be afraid to allow God to search you and know you in your prayer time with him. He is a loving father that want only what is best for his children.

When you take the time to pray you are fulfilling the scripture in your behalf. We are encouraged to tell God our concerns through our prayer time. Philippians tells us "Be careful for nothing; but in everything by prayer and supplication with thanksgiving let your request be made known unto God" (v.6). There is no reason for you to become anxious tell God your concerns and allow him to do what he feels is best but you must let him handle it. Be assured that he won't allow what he has purposed for you to go undone, for what he starts he completes. Again, Philippians can attest to this in the first chapter "Being confident of this very thing, that he which hath begun a good work in you will perform (complete) it until the day of Jesus Christ" (v.6).

Ask the Lord to help you be reminded that in whatever situation you are faced with, you will remember to pray. When you take the time to pray it is the best way to fight any problem. When you seek God in prayer it's speaking to who you trust for your victory.

Our fight is truly not a fight in the natural but of a spiritual nature. Ephesians 6:12 gives insight to the fact that all fights can't be fought with our fist. This scripture says, "For we wrestle not against flesh and blood, but against principalities, against powers, against the rulers of the darkness of this world, against spiritual wickedness in high places." This scripture also allows us to see that there are many areas of opposition, battles that can't be fought in the natural but through prayer. Our Heavenly Father hears and see and he will fight for us. The scripture says "For the eyes of the Lord run to and fro throughout the whole earth to show himself strong in the behalf of them whose heart is perfect toward him."(II Chronicles 16:9). As you take the time to pray you should also trust in his mercy. The Lord's eyes are upon those who also hope in his mercy, (Psalm 33:18).

It is important that we take the time to go to God in prayer because we many times can't see the things that are right in front of us therefore without the Lord's help we will enter areas of spiritual and natural danger. Therefore just as Elisha prayed to the Lord to open his servant's eyes we too need the Lord to open our eyes in a way that only God can (II King 6:15-17). Prayer is important to our very existence and God is waiting to meet you in prayer.

The decision to stop whatever you are doing and go to God in prayer is always your decision to make. Never be afraid to pray and never worry about how you should pray, just began to talk to God just as you would to anyone else, he understands you. There are no words that you may use that he does not understand the meaning of or what you mean by the words that you use. He wants your time the time that you are willing to set aside just for him. A time that nothing or no one else can share because you have made him a priority for that time. Also when you set aside that time to pray be willing to be open in your praying. Although God is a God that know all things still be willing to be transparent when you are praying to him. When you are willing to be transparent before the Lord, you are acknowledging that you truly believe there is nothing to hard for God. You are also saying that you want healing and/or deliverance in every area of your life.

In your prayer time if there is any inner turmoil or doubt as you release your request to God be reminded of Mark 9:24, it was a father's plea for his child. The desire for deliverance was there and Jesus said to him "If thou canst believe, all things are possible to him that believeth" (v.23). In verse 24, the father said with tears "Lord, I believe; help thou mine unbelief." I make mention of this scripture because there are times that in our praying, we wrestle with our faith to believe that we will receive all that we seek God for but just know that this does not mean you don't have faith it reminds you of the spiritual war you are in, and this is why we seek God in prayer. Just ask him to help your unbelief.

There are times when we all should ask of our Father, Lord, help my unbelief. Although there are some that may not want to acknowledge it, there comes times in our seeking the Lord in prayer that there is a wrestling in our spirit of what our results will be to the prayers that we have prayed and not only what the results will be but when our results will come. Again I say that it is not that we don't have faith but we wrestle in our in-between place and this is why it is important to take the time to pray. Trust God to do what He says he will do and that is to bring us to an expected end.

We each can have what we need from the Lord if we go into prayer with expectation from our Lord and Savior, Jesus Christ. Seek the Lord for His spirit to dwell within you. Listen to what will make the difference in every praying person "Now unto him that is able to do exceeding abundantly above all that we ask or think, according to the power that worketh in us" (Ephesians 3:20). It says according to the power that worketh in us. We need the Holy Ghost working in us, it is our power.

If there are areas of this chapter that you don't have the understanding you need, please go to the Lord in prayer and allow his spirit to give you understanding. He will do that for you. He is with you in your in-between place to take you through every storm that you will encounter. Take the time even now and seek him in prayer. Be sensitive to his spirit, allow it to give you what you need to take you through this place at this time and answer your unanswered questions and to bring you out on the other side of it all.

Pain and Forgiveness

The struggle that comes in an in-between place seem many times, as though there is no way out. It seems like you can hear the adversary saying to you, you won't make it to the other side, but you must be able to press into the spirit of prayer and know that the God you serve is able to do the seem like impossible thing. I said, the "seem like impossible thing" because Jesus said, "If thou canst believe, all things are possible (not impossible), to him that believeth" (Mark 9:23). You can't just, believe for a moment; make a practice of consistently believing God at His word. When the word of God says it that settles it. I once had a practice of saying, "God said it, and I believe it and that settles it". But there came a time when I open my mouth to make that statement and the Holy Spirit spoke to me, "God says it, that settles it." Oh praise God for His word and being led by His spirit. Give God praise again for who he is. God is the God that can't lie (Numbers 23:19).

As I think back on some of the struggles I have endured in my in-between place, it was the word of God that had been a constant for me. Scriptures such as "wait on the Lord: be of good courage, and he shall strengthen thine heart: wait, I say, on the Lord" (Psalm 27:14), helped me to realize that waiting on the Lord is important when you're struggling.

When you are struggling to cope with the pain and disappointments that sometimes present themselves in your life, you realize that waiting on the Lord is something that most people don't want to do, it becomes a struggle, but it is something that is needful many times. Many of our most difficult times are there to help us learn how to trust God through it all. We trust God because we love him and we know with everything that is within us, he loves us too. He love us so much that even in our most difficult and painful times he will not leave us to go through those times alone. Believing within yourself that Jesus will not leave you alone can cause a battle on its own. A battle because the adversary don't want you to stand on that belief but he want to put doubt in your mind. There are times when Christians say they trust the Lord but with every turn in their life they find themselves doubting whether or not He will be with them to bring them through their situation. Although Christians know that Jesus is the answer to whatever they may face in their in-between place, yet small forms of doubt brakes through. This is not the problem with every Christian but there are some that face this battle.

Doubt can brake through many times because the pain a person may face in this in-between place is more difficult than one could have ever imagine. There can be memories of times past when a person never completely got over them and these memories now show up at a time unexpected, a time that the person feels that it is too much to handle at that season in their life.

Many of us are unable to revisit some of the painful areas that is within us because we are afraid we can't get through some of the damage that is still there. Now, many of the things you may have thought you left behind will let you know that they are not dead but very much alive, invading you at every turn you make. It is at this moment, in this place, that the winds of your past began to blow, the waves began to toss high, and your ship of peace starts rocking and the enemy tells you that you have nothing else that you can hold on to.

Now, doubt speaks out and you hear yourself saying, "Master", carest not that I am perishing in this in-between place? The storms of my past are raging. It is at this point that you are able to realize that the things you thought you had put behind you through prayer and forgiveness is not gone but has been suppressed. What you hadn't realized was, although you worked hard at forgiving, you actually suppressed the pain that had caused scars and damaged the very core of your heart. You began to realize that deep down in your heart you had not allowed yourself to be healed and you were not healed, just numb.

The in-between place can be difficult many times because it is a challenge to how well you trust Jesus. Will you completely trust him or will you allow the spirit of doubt to come forth when the pain seem to be too great. Forgiveness can bring healing but if the pain is still deep down in a place that you didn't even realize was there then, there is something that is not completely forgiven. There is so much that we allow to hinder the call we have received from God to move forward in him. Many times things that people have done to cause you hurt and pain can also cause you to become stagnant in forgiveness and that pain of your past will let you know that all has not been forgiven and you are yet holding on to the pain.

Pain that is too difficult for you to release can cause you to become stuck in an in-between place. While you are yet stuck in your in-between place, if you will take the time to truly listen to the prayers you are praying and your cry to the Lord, you may hear your inner voice crying out to God wondering if he care that you can't seem to find your way out. But, if you will continue to hold on and keep trusting God you will be able to understand that God yet have a plan for your life.

As you are struggling in your in-between place, don't focus on where you are at the moment but where you are going. You must know for yourself where the Lord has told you to go. It is not your past or where you've been, it's not where you are now, it's your future, the place God has ordained for you to be. Struggles will cause you to press when you are determined to follow Jesus and be sure that you are following and have not become distracted by the fear of where you are at this present moment. Keep in mind that where you are at one moment may not be the place you will be the next moment. This is why, wherever Jesus has told you to go is the most important part of your follow-ship with him, and yes I meant to say follow-ship, not fellowship. Take the time to consider your relationship in following Jesus.

Jesus leads and you are to sweetly follow, trusting him all the way. Many times we become distracted where we are, forgetting where we are headed. It is important to keep fresh in your mind what the master has spoken, let's cross to the other side. Therefore, where you are is not as important as where you are headed. Where you are headed becomes encouraging as you keep the words of the master fresh in your heart. Remember that Jesus has already informed you that He know the plans he have for you and when his plans are fulfilled it will bring you to an expected end or future. It is in that assurance that you should be able to give him praise. Even now if you know within yourself there are things that have a painful effect, if you speak of them or think on them too much, then you need deliverance and you need it now. Go before God in prayer and ask him to help you forgive those that has hurt you and also to forgive you and set you free. If you are unsure how to go to God in prayer, just talk to God

the same way that you would talk to others. He will hear you, if you will speak and he will answer, I promise this is true. Don't allow the enemy to make you feel like you have been unfaithful to your relationship with Christ, it is untrue you didn't know how to completely forgive and release things to the Father and allow him to cleanse your hurt and pain.
Allow him to take away the very memory of what has been done to you and the affects it had on your life. It is possible for there to be total deliverance for the children of God. Forgiveness is not only for the one that has damaged you, but it is for you too. You have to be able to release the person or persons who had such an effect in your life. This forgiveness is for you also, that you may be able to continue serving God pain free of your past, Praise God.
God want you healed, he want you whole and complete just as he want others healed. You may be in an in-between place but you don't have to be or stay stuck there. God says in Isaiah 43:5 "Fear not; for I am with thee…" and in verse 19 it says, "Behold, I will do a new thing." God has a plan for your life as I have said before and he will not leave you stuck in your pain with no way of escape. Even now you should tell the Lord "thank you" don't let self, make you feel ashamed, tell God thank you and mean it. This is a God, a savior that has planned your deliverance even before you were born. Don't try to figure this out just accept it and be thankful. You

have purpose and you have a destiny, precious child of God, now tell him thank you again.

The book of Psalm says God inhabits your praise 22:3, and then Psalm 107:20-21 says, he sent his word and healed them, and delivered them from their destruction. Oh that men (and women) would praise the Lord for his goodness, and for his wonderful works to the children of men. This is the same God, and the same Savior that is right there with you healing and delivering your pain and you should be willing to give him praise, for He alone is worthy.

Begin to walk in your deliverance, your total forgiveness and know also that you have been totally forgiven. You walk in healing with the river of life flowing through you. Jesus says in Mark 9:23 "If thou canst believe, all things are possible to him (her) that believeth." This is your time, your season if you will believe, it is yours. Can you feel the healing virtue of the Most High God flowing through you? The spirit of God want us to be whole and complete. The spirit want you to know that you are free of pain, know it without any doubt. Doubt is of the enemy and it is a weapon that the enemy uses against you. Be free, my brother, my sister, be free. The hand and the spirit of the living God is doing great things for you and in you. Be free, be free, be free, it is done. You are free in the name of Jesus, now receive it. Allow the oil of joy to flow through you and from this point forward allow yourself to be dressed in the garment of praise. Be blessed in your going and in your coming. You have left the place called there to arrive at the place called here and you are moving forward to the destiny of God that is on the other side of your in-between place. Praise God, Hallelujah. The master has never and will never leave you in the middle of the journey he has you traveling. He is with you. If you can believe you can have just what you need.

Transformation

How many times have you said to yourself that you want change in your life? Maybe you are not even sure of what it is that you want changed, you just want things to be different. God want to bring a transformation in your life, to transform your circumstances if you will allow him to but it is up to you. God has a plan for your life that will cause you to become a vessel that is pleasing in his sight, a vessel of honor. To be this vessel there will be a transition that needs to take place and God will with every willing vessel, cause a transformation to take place in your life through a process that you go through one step at a time, one day at a time.

Your transformation will come through your process of changing. Being transitioned from the old you, the person that want things the way you think they should be. The way you feel good about because it may fit the way you see life. But, God wants to take your old condition, not a sinful condition but a comfortable condition. God wants to allow old conditions to be passed away and the new to take place; he wants to transition you through the process, through change. Transformation is like a metamorphosis taking place. It's the caterpillar be transformed into the butterfly. You don't see the entire process because the caterpillar weaves a cocoon that covers it while it go through its metamorphosis. You are like the caterpillar as you go through your process. God covers you as he take you through a transformation and you may not be able to see your changes that are taking place within you but you feel and know that you are being transitioned to something different.

Change is not always easy but as you began submitting to the Lord by seeking his will the cocoon began to be weaved. Praying to be sensitive to his voice you are weaving the cocoon. Jesus wants you to hear his voice and harden not your heart. Humble yourself under the mighty hand of God (I Peter 5:6). Once your spiritual cocoon has been woven metamorphosis began to take place because you have begun to take the steps to walk out the process.

Metamorphosis is an in-between place and you must stay in the cocoon until God determines your change has taken place. Acknowledging that God has a plan for your life and seeking to know his will is an important part of your transformation. You must allow your change to take place completely. You can't rush the process. The process of metamorphosis has to be walked out. Do you know exactly what to do every time, maybe not, but through prayerfully seeking God's will and staying sensitive to his spirit this will help you in the process. You take one step at a time, one day at a time before you can be presented a beautiful butterfly, one that has stood the test of time.

A butterfly don't come from its cocoon and have to go back in because it is not ready. When you can't go through the storms that come and you can't take rebuke or follow instructions your metamorphosis hasn't taken place. You may think that you are a butterfly but have you truly endured the process. It does not matter how hot the woven place may get, that caterpillar has to stay there until the transformation is complete, and it doesn't get angry or bitter but goes through its process. The caterpillar wants to come forth as a beautiful butterfly because that is its assignment. If that caterpillar will stay through the process it will no longer be that worm crawling around unable to fly. Seek God that you may know your assignment.

Every one of us has an assignment from the Lord but you have to seek out what that assignment is and when you want to know your assignment you will not allow anything to hinder you from seeking it out. It is easier to give reasons why you don't know your assignment or you can't follow through but this is only a trick sent to you from the enemy. God is greater than the enemy that has crossed your path designed to stop your process.

Transformation is a necessary process for my life in more ways than one and most likely more times than one. When the pains and heartaches find their way into my circumstances I take those same pains, and heartaches, both physical and spiritual to Christ, acknowledging that I need his help for my healing. His word helps me to know that he is concerned about me and what I am experiencing in that season of my life. I Peter says, "Casting all your care upon him; for he careth for you" (5:7). If you will allow yourself to be transparent and acknowledge that you are hurting and you are releasing your heartaches as well as any other pain that you are carrying but physically and spiritually, the Lord is willing and ready to heal your pain.

I try to always be transparent with my savior for he sees all and he know all therefore why try to hide anything from him. Christ is our deliverer and he is there to hear our cry and heal our pain. Deliverance is a part of the transformation that Christ want for his people but do you want that deliverance or do you believe that you need to be delivered in some areas of your life. A transformation will help you from becoming stagnant in a spiritually unproductive place.

A good way to be able to move forward is to ask God to help you take inventory of your life. Seek to know, through his spirit, the things that slow your spiritual progress in order to repent and allow God to bring a shift in your life. He wants to take each of us higher, to transform our external as well as our inward man. If you will just allow yourself to long for the change that Christ want to bring in you, to feel his touch moving in your spirit, causing you to become stronger day by day as you hunger for the more of him. If you hunger and thirst for him he will fill you with the more.

Jesus in his teaching on the mountain wanted to deal with the heart and the mind of his disciples, this same Jesus, our Lord and savior want to allow us the same opportunity to have the greatest of his blessings. Therefore Jesus says "Blessed are they which do hunger and thirst after righteousness: for they shall be filled" (Matthew 5:6). This is a transformation that the Lord wants all people to have not just a few, he said "blessed are they" anyone that truly have a hunger and a thirst for this change can have it. He also said "they shall" which means it has to happen because he can't lie. Now it is up to you to search your inner man and determine if you really want the change that is there in the savior just for you.

Allow yourself to be transformed, to go from level to level in the things of the Lord and recognize that as you are moving forward a greater transformation is taking place. Don't get stuck on a transformation but be open to the many transformations that await you. As I have said allowing yourself to go from level to level will allow a transformation to take place with each level. As life is changing you must be willing to change with the changes taking place in your process. Don't get stuck in an in-between place.

Hopefully with some insight of the caterpillar and the butterfly you have been able to recognize that things can be different in your life you have to be willing to allow God to let you know when it is time for a transformation in your life. When the caterpillar recognized it was time for its transformation it didn't fight the timing of God it just began to spin the silk like material that would weave its cocoon. The willing caterpillar spun the silk of its cocoon until it was no longer visible to those around it. Although others could no longer see the caterpillar they were aware that a caterpillar must be there because they could see its cocoon.

Being covered and protected by its cocoon the caterpillar was ready for the transformation that was to take place. The caterpillar went into its cocoon one way recognizing it would emerge forever changed by the hand of the Lord, never to be the same again. Therefore without fear or hesitation the caterpillar spun its cocoon willingly yielding to the transformation.

This is what God want for his people, to bring them into a change known as transformation that they will never be the same again. You can't be afraid you must be willing. When David said to God create in me a clean heart…renew a right spirit within me (Psalm 51:10), David knew that only God could do this for him because only God could reach into the heart of a man and clean it. Also knowing that the spirit is not a tangible thing therefore it takes God to do the work David was seeking from God with his request. It's like David wanted God to reach into his spiritual cocoon and transform him again.

You must realize that it takes God to reach pass your flesh (cocoon) into your spirit to bring transformation; man can't penetrate your spiritual cocoon. Oh how grate is our God, a God that is worthy to be praised, hallelujah. There is no need for fear the only need is the need to submit to the master that is waiting to change you into the beautiful butterfly that you have been created to be.

When the caterpillar began to weave its cocoon it only had the ability to crawl, if you threw it into the air it would only fall to the ground. But during the caterpillar's time in its cocoon being transformed by God many things changed and God knew that mere caterpillar would never be the same. Scripture tells us "…if any man be in Christ, he is a new creature (creation): old things are passed away; behold, all things are become new." II Corinthians 5:17).

The caterpillar not only emerged from its cocoon looking different but its abilities were different; when it went into the cocoon it was only able to crawl but it emerged with the ability to fly. When the caterpillar went into the cocoon it was wingless but it emerged with beautiful, colorful wings. When it wove itself in it was known as the caterpillar but when it emerged it was called the butterfly. Only Christ has the power to not only change your name but to change your abilities also. You may go in as old but come forth a new creature in Christ. Don't stay a mere worm, allow Christ to bring out the butterfly that is within you.

You must know also that it has been said, concerning the butterfly, that when the butterfly is ready to come forth once the wings of the butterfly has been formed they must be able to fly. Just think, when the wings of the butterfly is formed do they have the strength to fly? If not, how do they gain the strength they need to come forth flying? This transformation of the worm to the butterfly is not about trial and error.

Listen to what Apostle Paul has to say about gaining the strength that he needed. Paul had situations and weak areas in his life and he wanted these things removed for which he went to Jesus. Now just in case you feel like Jesus will remove every obstacle out of your way this is Jesus' response to Apostle Paul, "My grace is sufficient for thee: for my strength is made perfect in weakness. Most gladly therefore will I rather glory (says Paul) in my infirmities, that the power of Christ may rest upon me. Therefore I take pleasure in infirmities, in reproaches, in necessities, in persecutions, in distresses for Christ's sake: for when I am weak then am I strong" (II Corinthians 12:9-10).

This scripture is a good example of ruff things that could be seen as designs sat up to stop progress, but God. You see, the butterfly once it is complete in its transformation now must be free to fly. The butterfly's flight depends on its wings but the wings that has never flown need strength to mount up in flight. Can God speak and the butterfly come forth and start flying, yes. But God has a process and it is your process that is designed to transform you.

Now back to the butterfly. Once the butterfly is ready to come forth it begins to rub its wings against the inside of the cocoon where he is. Back and forth, back and forth the butterfly rubs its wings. Although he is weak, now he is becoming strong. Not only does the wings of the butterfly gain strength but it also thins out the wall of the cocoon that is holding the butterfly in, this is not easy but this is process. After a period of time in the process of rubbing his wings against the cocoon's inner wall the butterfly has an opening and the strength to come forth and fly. He was weak but through process, he was made strong. Now a beautiful butterfly emerges with beautiful colorful strong wings flying for all to see. Just think, you might look upon yourself as just a mere worm but if you will allow Jesus to ride with you through his process of an in-between place, you too can come forth as a beautiful butterfly with the strength and the ability to fly beyond your circumstances. Fly butterfly, fly and be blessed.

Crossing to the Other Side

Although we may continue to find ourselves in some form of an in-between place, God delivers us from many of these places but you just may find yourselves entering others. Jesus is calling you to come forth and let's go to the other side. When Jesus said, let us go to the other side, this say's to you when he used the term *us,* that he was going to be with you as you crossed to the other side. Why should anyone that truly love the Lord and believe that he truly love them, worry when you know that someone that love you want you to travel with him. If Jesus has the ability to walk on the water without fear, he is able to sustain you. Therefore you must be able to recognize who is traveling with you.

Jesus loves each of us, he love you and me. This is why he gave his life for you and for me. He died that we may be able to have a redeemed life and walk in salvation with the assurance that one day we will be able to truly arrive at the other side of it all, never to be in an in-between place again. But, be it known dear people of God until that time, know that storms will come and storms will go. You may find yourself in and out of in-between places but please be reminded that Jesus is able to keep you from drowning in your storm and he will keep you from falling overboard your ship of life if you are willing to hold on and trust him to bring you out of your storm. If you are willing to obey what the Lord instructs you to do through his word and his anointing, according to your faith, the deliverance that you seek shall be yours. When Jesus speaks so shall it be, unto you.

Jesus has never lied nor will he ever therefore, when Jesus says come, let us go to the other side, go. Just think, Jesus said to Peter when he ask Jesus, bid me to come to thee on the water, Jesus said come, and Peter went. Know who it is that you decide to ask something of when you are crossing to the other side of your circumstances.

When you are crossing to the other side of your in-between place don't be like Lot's wife (Gen.19:26) and look back, but learn to walk in obedience to what the Lord has said to you and leave your past and all that it may entail behind you, keep looking forward. When you choose to look back you will lose sight of what is before you and one spiritual second can make the difference in reaching your goal or running into something that can cause you to feel like you are sinking.

It is important to make right choices of what you will keep in your view while you are crossing or going through your in-between place. The winds of your mind can blow strong as you press toward that mark called the other side. The other side of your disappointments, the other side of mistrust and confusion, also the other side of so many wrong choices. You are already aware of the fact that you have to leave behind some things that have been with you for a long time. You are crossing now and everything that you use to have can't go with you because there are too many. Too many thoughts, too many memories of how things use to be, are weighing at your soul. There are too many friends that don't want the things that you want for your life in Christ. Understand that your spiritual ship will only allow for so many things. Therefore you keep yourself prepared for crossing by getting rid of the weights. Hebrews says, "...let us lay aside every weight, and the sin which doth so easily beset us..." (12:1). It is not always easy to turn away or lay aside things that have become a part of you but if you intend to get to the other side it is a choice that you will have to make.

As you ride the waves of your in-between place keep in mind that you are not alone, the master of your soul is with you. There are times we have to keep reminding ourselves of the promises that Jesus has already given to us at the beginning of our journey which is "be content with such things as ye have...I will never leave thee, nor forsake thee"(Heb. 13:5). We have the Lord's promise and that should be enough. It is when we are not content with the things God has given us that we have a problem in crossing to the other side.

It is necessary to cross to the other side because the Lord goes with you. This in-between place to the other side is not there to stop you but to assure you. It assures those that go through, to trust God at his word and learn contentment with Jesus because he is the master also of the sea. You may be tossed but you won't die, trust God.

When Paul was sent as a prisoner to Rome, in between Paul's much traveling he encountered winds and storms that seemed as though they might destroy the ship that Paul was traveling in, but God. God assured Paul that he would not be harmed, the ship may break up because of the storms but Paul and those that sailed with him would not be harmed (Acts 27). As Paul sat sail for Rome he entered an in-between place. Take time to notice that Paul's storm came as he made steps to leave from the place he was in, although he was a prisoner, and moved forward to another. A storm from the enemy is designed to stop you but you have to keep reminding yourself that you are not alone; the master is on board with you. Paul knew that God was with him because God has sent an angel to minister to him before he sat sail and Paul held on to the words of the Lord and although the others didn't believe him, he chose to believe God (v 25).

Paul arrived at the other side, ship broke up, supplies loss, and nothing surrounding them, they had to swim because the ship was no longer whole. But, God did just what he said he would do; he did not allow Paul and those that were with him to be harmed. Although on that ship Paul was a prisoner, he was freer than anyone on the ship. The captain and all the soldiers were saved from the storm because Paul was on board and God had need of Paul arriving at Rome safely. Recognize that Paul did not arrive at Rome trouble free, but God was God with Paul in his in-between place and he didn't leave Paul when the storm came.

Just as God was with Paul in his in-between place, instructing him and encouraging him, this same God, Jesus, your Lord and Savior, will be with you. Where the spirit of the Lord is there is liberty (II Cor. 3:17). Therefore, remember that while you are in your in-between place, crossing to the other side, God is with you. The wind, wave, and whatever storm the enemy send can't stop you from going to the place that God has ordained you to be.

While crossing to the other side you must be able to allow God to speak into your spirit, and by his spirit, give you the ability to envision all the things He has for you. The things that God has already placed in your future as he prepared his plan for your life is waiting just for you on the other side of your in-between place. As you are crossing to the other side allow God to help you to see (envision) in your future (the other side) and see what no one else has been able to see. Only God can give you the ability to envision your future in his will. When God allow you to see vision by revealing his will to you, you must understand that you have been able to adhere to divine revelation straight from God. God told the prophet Habakkuk "Write the vision, and make it plain...the vision is yet for an appointed time..."(Habakkuk 2:2-3). Everything God does is for an appointed time therefore, it is important to be sensitive to the spirit of God and how God want to move in your relationship with him. It is good that you have a desire to see what God want you to see and to know what he want you to know at this season in your life of crossing to the other side, as well as this time of deliverance from your in-between place.

For many the in-between place is a place that is not understood. The process of the in-between is a good place. Sometimes it is a place that you can steal away with the master. But because of the fear that the traveler holds on to, it becomes a place unwanted by most of the followers. Don't allow fear to cause you to miss an appointed time to be alone with the master. A time to share and pour out your heart to him. A time to receive instructions or gain encouragement. Maybe this could be your time to gain insight into the will of God for your future. Just think about at this time, it is just you and the savior, alone without any interruptions, what an opportunity. But, notice how quick things can change.

Jesus had spent much time with his disciples, teaching them through parables, and now it was time to leave the multitude behind and move forward. At Jesus' word to cross to the other side, and the disciples' obedience to follow, a storm arose. The sea was alright, calm, before Jesus started into this in-between place going to the other side. Of all the training, long hours of teaching, as Jesus moved from the banks of the shore a storm arose and this first storm caused fear to arise in the disciples and it was not just fear but Jesus' followers questioned his love and concern for them. Jesus had just invited them to an in-between place with him and their response was not the master is with us, instead their response was "Master, carest thou not that we perish?" (Mark 4:38). How quickly had they forgotten the things Jesus had taught them during their time with him?

Life with its winds and waves can make one forget their time spent with Jesus. The spirit of fear can make you lose sight on the teachings of the master that was given to you through his spirit. Tribulations is one of the things that will help you to recognize if you have learned all that you think you have. Fear is powerful whether you perceive it to be or not, but hear what the scripture has said, "For God hath not given us the spirit of fear; but of power, and of love, and of a sound mind" (II Timothy 1:7).

Although fear is a powerful spirit the people of God has power also over the enemy therefore we should never question the love or concern of the master for his followers. Life's storms are not for you to question the care of your savior but to humble yourself under the mighty hand of God (I Peter 5:6), and to know that be it storm or calm he will never leave you nor forsake you (Hebrew 13:5). The only power that fear has over the true followers of God is the power that you give to fear.

Take time to stop and think clearly, through prayer and meditation to through prayer and meditation, allow yourself to be ministered to through the word of God and the spirit of God. This within itself is a process and your in-between place is the part of that process that will strengthen you and equip you for what awaits you on the other side. When you arrive to the other side, if you have moved through your in-between place trusting the Lord, you should have reached another level in your walk with Christ. Something is out of place if you are going through different storms, spiritually, and do not learn from those storms how to get through them and not become consumed by them. Your in-between place is a vital part of the process that takes you to the other side.

There must be an understanding while going through this in-between place that you may now be in, when you arrive at the other side, there will be another in-between place and there will always be other sides to each of your in-between places that are designed to continue taking you through the process of getting you to the place that God has prepared just for you. You can't have the mentality of being in an in-between place and then you get to the other side and that's it, life is much more than that.

David had many in-between places and experiences to go through so that he could arrive at the many other sides that God had planned for his life. This was designed to help David arrive at the many other sides that God had planned to elevate David to a place in God that he wanted David to arrive at, equipped. For David the flocks of sheep took David through an in-between place to arrive at a lion on the other side. It was the strengthening of an in-between place that helped David to arrive at the other side of a bear, and David's in-between place equipped him to have victory over the lion and the bear. You must understand that it was not the end of David's in-between experience because David had an encounter with another, other side, experience that seem real good, he experienced being anointed king. Every in-between place does not mean trouble because God has a plan for you just as he had for David. On the other side of David being anointed as king was King Saul with an evil spirit and David's in-between place was yet equipping and strengthening him to meet and defeat the giant Goliath on the other side. There were many in-between experiences for David, many, but there were also experiences on some of the other sides that were such blessings that it brought David into covenant with God. While David was experiencing one of his in-between places, he was praying and talking with God and beheld Bath-sheba on the other side of where he was. David's encounter with Bath-sheba caused him to also encounter a Nathan that would send David back into an in-between place of repentance and sorrow but as the word of God says "…all things work together for good to them that love God, to them who are the called according to his purpose" (Romans 8:28). Therefore be it known that every in-between place and every other side is not bad but it is working for the good in you when you love God. You must stand still long enough to see that God has purpose for your life and he wants to work good in you, that he get the glory.

If there is no other understanding that you gain from this chapter just know that your travel through the place called in-between is the process of equipping you to cross to the other side. Every experience within the in-between and the other side is always working to bring you to the plan that God has for your life and that plan is for good and not evil. God's plan and his thoughts for you are of peace therefore don't fear just trust the Lord for the process.

You can't go by what you see, the process is not based on what you can see with your natural eyes, but instead on what you can trust God to do through his love and his care for you in the spirit. Remember what Jesus' disciples said when they were looking through natural eyes, "Master, carest thou not that we perish?" (Mark 4:38). Many times what you see in the natural will cause you to fear and fear will cause you to doubt and doubt gives the enemy a weapon to use against you. You just might be the Esther that God want to use at this season of your life to travel the in-between place with the mindset that I'm going through this place, winds blowing, waves raging, ship shaking, and "if I perish, I perish" (Esther 4:16b), but I will cross to the other side. Even when your mind want you to think that everything is working against you in this in-between place and the enemy want you to think that you have nothing left, be bold enough to say as Job said "though he slay me, yet will I trust in him…"(Job 13:15a). When you make up your mind to trust God with all, although you don't always understand why things are the way they are you can say like Mary "...be it unto me according to thy word…"(Luke 1:38). It is not about understanding God's will, but being obedient to his will.

I encourage you as you are in your in-between places, crossing to the other side and the adversary want to try and bring the spirit of fear and doubt upon you, that you continue to remind yourself that your Heavenly Father does not want you to fear. Refresh your mind with thoughts of scripture such as Luke 12:32, which says "Fear not, little flock; for it is your Father's good pleasure to give you the kingdom." This scripture alone should encourage you because it pleases God to give you the kingdom therefore if you will continue to remind yourself as I have asked you earlier, you would not question whether your Savior love and care for you or not. Whatever is awaiting you on the other side is there for your good.

There is no Goliath big and strong enough to defeat the God (Holy Ghost) in you, for you have been placed in your in-between place for such a time as this, someone on the other side is watching you come through your in-between place because there is a process that is awaiting them also that is called in-between that they too must go through. Now it is up to you to make up your mind and say to yourself, I won't get stuck where I am, and I refuse to go back to where I've been. I'm going to the other side. Be blessed, the Master is in the ship with you and how great is our God, a wonderful Savior is He.

www.ingramcontent.com/pod-product-compliance
Lightning Source LLC
Chambersburg PA
CBHW060525100426
42743CB00009B/1430